GRAMMAR AND BEYOND

WORKBOOK

Kathryn O'Dell

3A

CAMBRIDGE
UNIVERSITY PRESS

CAMBRIDGE
UNIVERSITY PRESS

University Printing House, Cambridge CB2 8BS, United Kingdom

One Liberty Plaza, 20th Floor, New York, NY 10006, USA

477 Williamstown Road, Port Melbourne, VIC 3207, Australia

314–321, 3rd Floor, Plot 3, Splendor Forum, Jasola District Centre, New Delhi – 110025, India

79 Anson Road, #06–04/06, Singapore 079906

Cambridge University Press is part of the University of Cambridge.

It furthers the University's mission by disseminating knowledge in the pursuit of education, learning and research at the highest international levels of excellence.

www.cambridge.org
Information on this title: www.cambridge.org/9781107601987

© Cambridge University Press 2012

First published 2012

20 19 18 17 16 15 14 13 12 11 10 9 8 7 6

Printed in Great Britain by CPI Group (UK) Ltd, Croydon CR0 4YY

A catalogue record for this publication is available from the British Library

ISBN 978-0-521-14298-4 Student's Book 3
ISBN 978-0-521-14315-8 Student's Book 3A
ISBN 978-0-521-14319-6 Student's Book 3B
ISBN 978-1-107-60197-0 Workbook 3
ISBN 978-1-107-60198-7 Workbook 3A
ISBN 978-1-107-60199-4 Workbook 3B
ISBN 978-1-107-68502-4 Teacher Support Resource Book with CD-ROM 3
ISBN 978-0-521-14339-4 Class Audio CD 3
ISBN 978-1-139-06187-2 Writing Skills Interactive 3

Art direction and layout services: Integra

Contents

PART 3 The Future

PART 4 Modals and Modal-like Expressions

PART 5 Nouns and Pronouns

PART 6 Gerunds and Infinitives

Simple Present and Present Progressive

First Impressions

Simple Present vs. Present Progressive

1 Complete the article with the words in parentheses. Use the simple present or present progressive. Sometimes more than one answer is possible.

Teacher of the Year

This month in our newsletter we *are profiling* (profile)
(1)
different teachers at Summerville Community College. Kevin

Lewis, a grammar teacher, was recently voted "Teacher of the

Year" here at Summerville. We interviewed some of the students

who voted for him to find out the reasons they think he is a really

effective teacher. Here are some of the things they said. "Mr. Lewis _____
(2)
(treat) all students fairly. He _____ (explain) everything carefully. He
(3)
_____ (not lose) his patience. This week, during exams, he
(4)
_____ (keep) extended office hours to help the students who need
(5)
extra help. He _____ (always / tell) students to feel free to
(6)
drop in to talk with him when they _____ (see) him in his office. He
(7)
_____ (always / make) a good impression on the first day of
(8)
class by dressing nicely, speaking clearly, and learning all the students' names. Mr. Lewis

respects the students, and we _____ (respect) him."
(9)
We also interviewed Mr. Lewis. Here are some of the things he had to say. "I

really like teaching. I _____ (wake up) every morning excited about
(10)
my classes. I _____ (teach) several classes this semester, but I
(11)
_____ (always / try) to be available for my students during
(12)
class and outside the classroom, too. Also, I think it's important to keep my students

motivated, so I _____ (constantly / look) for ways to make my
(13)
classes more interesting and enjoyable."

2 Complete the sentences about a professor's research study. Use the words in parentheses with the simple present or present progressive.

1. Dr. Andrei Baronova __is__ (be) a professor of psychology.

2. He _____ (not teach) classes this semester.

3. Instead, he _____ (do) research on stress.

4. Specifically, he _____ (investigate) "test anxiety."

5. Some of his students from last semester _____ (participate) in

   this research, but others _____ (not work) with him.

6. He _____ (typically / meet) with these students once a week.

7. They _____ (often / talk) about their feelings during exams.

8. Dr. Baronova _____ (usually / ask) them specific questions.

9. At the moment, he _____ (ask) them questions about

   their "self-talk"[1] during exams because he believes that a lot of students

   _____ (generally / say) negative things to themselves.

10. At the same time, he _____ (also / teach) them how to use

    positive self-talk, not negative self-talk.

[1]**self-talk:** what people say to themselves, for example, "I can't do this" (negative) and "I can do this" (positive)

3 Complete the telephone conversation. Use the simple present or present progressive with the words in parentheses. Use contractions when possible.

Kazuki: Hi, Meena? It's Kazuki. What _are you doing_ (do)?

(1)

Meena: Hi, Kazuki. I _____ (walk) to class. How about you?

(2)

Kazuki: Oh, I _____ (study) right now, but I'll need to relax later.

(3)

   _____ you _____ (want) to go to the movies

(4) (4)

   tonight?

Meena: _____ the new Daniel Craig and Rooney Mara movie still

(5)

   _____ (play)?

(5)

Kazuki: No. It _____ (not play) at the local theater anymore, but

(6)

   they _____ (show) *First and Last Impressions.*

(7)

Meena: Oh, I _____ (want) to see that. What time does it start?

(8)

Kazuki: It _____ (start) at 6:15. Let's meet there at 6:00.

(9)

Meena: Great! See you then.

Stative Verbs

1 Greg is going to meet the parents of Rachel, the woman he is going to marry. Circle the correct forms of the verbs to complete the conversation. Remember that some verbs, such as *be*, *think*, and *have*, can have stative or action meanings.

Alex: Greg, are you nervous about meeting your fiancée's parents tonight?

Greg: Very! Rachel **says** / **is saying** they're great people, but right now **I have / I'm having**
    (1)   (2)
trouble remembering that because I'm so nervous. My hands are shaking.

Alex: Really? You **don't seem / aren't seeming** nervous.
                      (3)

Greg: Well, I'm glad **I look / I'm looking** fine, anyway.
                        (4)

Alex: **Do you think / Are you thinking** about how to make a good first impression?
          (5)

Greg: Yeah.

Alex: You **don't have / aren't having** anything to worry about. You need to relax!
               (6)

Greg: Thanks. I'm sure you're probably right. I guess **I'm / I'm being** silly. Hey,
                                                         (7)
do you hear / are you hearing something? I think they're here!
    (8)

Alex: Relax. It's not a job interview. They're probably nervous, too.

Greg: Well, **it feels / it's feeling** like a stressful interview for a really important job!
                (9)
I really want / I'm really wanting to make a good first impression.
    (10)

Alex: Well, I guess **I need / I'm needing** to go now! **I don't think / I'm not thinking**
                        (11)   (12)
I should be here when you meet them. Good luck!

2 Complete each pair of sentences with the simple present and present progressive forms of the same verb. Use the words in bold. In one sentence, the verb has a stative meaning. In the other sentence, the same verb has an action meaning.

be Jeff _is_ in a new town and doesn't know many people yet. This month he
(1)

_____ adventurous and trying an online dating service.
(2)

have He knows that some people who use online

dating websites _____ good
(3)

luck. Right now he _____ only
(4)

bad luck ...

see Maybe the problem is that he always

_____ the imperfections in
(5)

people, so it's hard for him to find a good

match. At the moment, he _____ a woman he met at the grocery store.
(6)

think Jeff _____ about joining a hiking club, too. He _____ that
(7)   (8)

might be a good way to meet new people, make friends, and get some exercise, too.

Special Meanings and Uses of Simple Present

1 Complete the article about "love at first sight." Use the simple present of the verbs in parentheses.

_Do_ you _believe_ (believe) in love at first sight?
(1)   (1)

Some people _____ (say) that
(2)

they recognized their true love from the very first

time they met. We _____ (be)
(3)

all familiar with stories like these: A man

_____ (see) a woman across
(4)

a room, and he immediately _____ (recognize) his soul mate.[1] A woman
(5)

_____ (hear) a man's voice, and she _____ (feel) an instant
(6)   (7)

attraction.

---
[1]**soul mate:** the perfect person for another person to marry

Some people may think, however, that these stories _____ (seem)
                                                                    (8)
more like fantasy than real life. They believe that some couples _____ even
                                                                          (9)

_____ (not like) each other at first, but then fall in love later.
          (9)

In fact, some people _____ (think) that couples who fall in love quickly
                            (10)

are the same couples who end their relationships quickly. On the other hand, couples

who _____ (not have) an instant attraction take time to get to know each
              (11)

other as friends. However, the best stories _____ (make) us believe in the
                                                        (12)

magic of love.

2 Complete the review of a book about intuition.[1] Use the simple present form of the verbs in
the box. Use each verb only once.

believe	give	live	say	travel
~~form~~	have	not pay	teach	use

We all _form_ first impressions when we use new products, go to new places, and meet
        (1)

new people. We sometimes call these impressions or feelings "gut reactions," and our

intuition or instinct[2] causes them. Some people _____ that intuition is very
                                                              (2)

important and can help us live better lives. Shannon Healy is one such person.

Healy is a strong believer that all people have natural powers of intuition. In her book, she

_____ that most people, however, _____ enough attention
          (3)   (4)

to their "gut feelings."

Her new book, *Use Your Intuition*, is full of stories of people who _____
                                                                                  (5)

their intuition to find love and success. For example, a young woman makes a quick

decision between two job offers. She chooses one by paying attention to her "gut feeling"

that she will enjoy the work more, even though the pay is lower. It turns out to be a

good choice. Each chapter of Healy's book _____ a specific focus, such
                                                      (6)

as love, work, children, or health. The exercises in the book _____ people
                                                                          (7)

practice on how to use their intuition to have success in all these areas.

_____

[1]**intuition:** a quick sense of what is true or right | [2]**instinct:** a natural sense of what to do

Occasionally, Healy also _____ students about using the power of
                                        (8)
intuition in workshops where she _____ – in Jacksonville, Florida. Some
                                            (9)
people _____ hundreds of miles to attend her workshops. *Use Your Intuition*
            (10)
is already a bestseller!

Avoid Common Mistakes

1 Circle the mistakes.

1. Even animals **seem** to form first impressions. I'm sure you have noticed they usually
         (a)
   (are reacting) quickly when they **meet** a new person.
         (b)   (c)

2. **Do you think** instincts have anything to do with first impressions?
      (a)
   Are we demonstrate animal behavior when we **have** strong reactions to new people?
            (b)   (c)

3. Most people **don't make** strong impressions on me. Sometimes I **forget** their
                    (a)   (b)
   names almost immediately. However, I often **am having** strong reactions to different
                                                  (c)
   geographic locations immediately.

4. Appearances **are** important the first time you **are meeting** someone. Everyone knows
                  (a)   (b)
   that you **look** better if you are dressed nicely and if you smile.
              (c)

5. Right now, our new salesman **is making** a good first impression on everyone at the
                                    (a)
   meeting. He **is stand** straight, and he **is looking** at everyone there.
                  (b)   (c)

6. Some parents **are believing** that schools should **teach** children social skills.
                    (a)   (b)
   They **feel** that making a good impression and working well in a group are very
          (c)
   important.

7. **I'm not have** a good time at this party. I **think** the food is bad and the music **is**
         (a)   (b)   (c)
   too loud.

8. I **want** to look good at my sister's wedding, so I **try** to lose weight this month.
       (a)   (b)
   I **think** that I need to lose about eight pounds.
       (c)

2 Find and correct eight more mistakes in the journal entry by a salesperson about making a good impression.

For salespeople, physical appearance is important, but there are other things that also

go into making a good first impression. For example, I always ~~am arriving~~ *arrive* at meetings

on time. I am knowing my clients are busy people, and I understand that their time is

important. Also, I always call them by name. I even keep names and information about

5 clients in a special file online. In fact, I add information to that file this week.

In the past, I didn't pay much attention to body language. However, I am learn to be

more conscious of the ways I move and how to use my hands effectively. At every meeting

I am making eye contact – especially when I first greet a client and again when I leave.

I practice my greetings in front of the mirror every day. I try to remember to smile. Of

10 course, I also want to look good. I have nice shoes, and I keep them clean and polished. I

am thinking my new haircut makes me look good, too.

My sales numbers used to be a bit low, but they go up now. I am try to do better. I am

knowing that I can be "Number One" in sales next year.

Self-Assessment

Circle the word or phrase that correctly completes each sentence.

1. Some top salespeople _____ their greetings and handshakes before they meet their customers.

   a. are practicing   b. practice   c. practices

2. Jack _____ a lot of success as a salesman this year.

   a. is not having   b. has not   c. doesn't have

3. I need to get a suit for my job interview. A nice suit _____ about $300.00 at Guys' Clothing.

   a. costs   b. is costing   c. cost

4. Some people _____ in love the moment they first meet each other.

   a. falls   b. are falling   c. fall

5. I _____ enough money for a haircut even though I really need one.

   a. don't having   b. 'm not having   c. don't have

6. Many animals depend on smell to form a first impression. They _____ as dependent on sight as people are.

   a. are   b. are not   c. are not being

7. I _____ parties where I don't know anyone.

   a. don't like   b. 'm liking   c. 'm not liking

8. _____ you _____ people's names immediately after you meet them?

   a. Do . . . using   b. Do . . . use   c. Are . . . use

9. What kinds of behavior _____ you _____ are the most damaging at a job interview?

   a. do . . . think   b. do . . . thinking   c. are . . . thinking

10. When Louisa takes a test, she decides which questions are the easiest. She answers those first, and then she answers the harder questions. Finally, she _____ all her answers one more time.

    a. reviews   b. is reviewing   c. review

11. A successful businessperson usually _____ on a positive attitude, hard work, and intuition.

    a. depends   b. depend   c. is depending

12. How do we _____ the success of a first meeting with someone else?

    a. measure   b. measures   c. measuring

13. The job fair _____ at 10:00 a.m.

    a. not open   b. opens   c. opening

14. This week, Bob _____ his salespeople a new way to make a better first impression.

    a. is teaching   b. teaching   c. teaches

15. Those salespeople _____ a very good first impression on the customers right now. Most of the customers are ignoring them as much as possible.

    a. don't make   b. aren't make   c. aren't making

Simple Past and Past Progressive; *Used To, Would*

Global Marketing

Simple Past vs. Past Progressive

1 Complete the article about one candy company's success. Use the simple past or past progressive form of the verbs in parentheses. Sometimes more than one answer is possible.

In 1982 *E.T.: The Extra-Terrestrial* <u>was</u> (be) a success for the movie company that
(1)

produced it – and it was also successful for a candy company. Here's what happened:

In the story, E.T. was an alien from outer space. He _____ (hide) in
(2)

the forest for a short time after his spaceship _____ (leave) Earth
(3)

without him. A young boy _____ (see) E.T. and decided to take him
(4)

home. The boy _____ (drop) pieces of candy on the ground all the
(5)

way to his house. He _____ (want) E.T. to follow the pieces of candy. It
(6)

worked. E.T. _____ (go) to the boy's house, and they became friends.
(7)

For a while, the movie company _____ (plan) to use a product
(8)

from another candy company. However, this company was not sure if it wanted its candy

in the film, and it _____ (take) some time to decide. When that candy
(9)

company _____ (say) no, another company _____
(10)   (11)

(offer) its candy for the film. It was a newer product and not famous yet. As soon

as the movie came out, movie theaters were not only selling lots of tickets, they

_____ (sell) lots of the new candy, too. The sales of the new candy
(12)

went up dramatically.

2 Complete the sentences about a garage sale.[1] Circle the correct form of the verbs.

1. My neighbors **got** / (**were getting**) ready to move to another city, so they (**decided**) / **were deciding** to have a garage sale.

    GARAGE SALE
    Saturday
    7:00 a.m.–3:00 p.m.
    78 Elm St.

2. Because they were hoping to have a very successful sale, they **did** / **were doing** a little online research.

3. They soon **realized** / **were realizing** that effective advertising is a very important part of a successful sale.

4. They **placed** / **were placing** one small ad in the local newspaper and one online.

5. They **made** / **were making** signs and **placed** / **were placing** them around the neighborhood.

6. They **used** / **were using** "word of mouth" advertising[2] by telling all their friends and neighbors.

7. People **began** / **were beginning** to arrive at 6:30 a.m. for the sale. My neighbors **still got** / **were still getting** everything ready.

8. At 3:05 p.m. a car full of people **parked** / **was parking** in front of the house. Too late!

9. My neighbors **already counted** / **were already counting** their money from the sale and **put** / **were putting** unsold items in boxes to give to charity at that time.

10. The people were disappointed, but they **understood** / **were understanding** that they had come too late.

---

[1]**garage sale:** a sale of used household items (furniture, books, dishes, clothes) usually held in the front yard or garage of the house | [2]**"word of mouth" advertising:** an informal recommendation of a product between people

3 Answer the questions. Use the simple past or past progressive. Write sentences that are true for you.

1. Did you ever sell anything when you were younger? What did you sell?

    _____

2. Did you ever advertise anything when you were younger? How did you advertise it?

    _____

3. What product made in another country did you buy this year?

    _____

4. What were you looking for the last time you went shopping?

    _____

5. Who were you shopping with the last time you went shopping?

    _____

Time Clauses with Simple Past and Past Progressive

1 Each sentence describes two past events. Underline the words that describe the first event.

1. As soon as <u>Empire Clothing opened a store in Brazil</u>, they realized that they didn't understand the local culture very well.

2. Before they hired a Brazilian marketing expert to improve their image there, business was terrible.

3. Once the expert began talking with their marketing department, business began to improve.

4. Everyone relaxed a little when sales increased.

5. The marketing expert continued to work with the company until they learned how to adapt their advertising to the local culture.

2 Complete the paragraph about an advertising experiment. Use the words in the box. Sometimes more than one answer is possible.

after	as soon as	~~before~~	once	until	while

<u>Before</u> he did his famous experiment in 1957, James
(1)
Vicary was a little-known researcher who studied the

shopping habits of women. In his 1957 experiment, Vicary

said he flashed two different messages on the movie

screen _____ the film *Picnic* was playing.
(2)
Each message was on the screen for only a fraction of a

second, too short a time for anyone to actually "see" the message, and it appeared every

few seconds. One message said to drink a famous kind of soda, and the other one said

to eat popcorn. Vicary reported that sales of the famous soda went up 18.1 percent and

sales of popcorn went up 57.8 percent immediately _____ people watched
(3)
the film. _____ people heard about these amazing results, they became
(4)
worried about the power of what Vicary called subliminal[1] advertising. Vicary was

quite famous _____ other researchers repeated this study. They found *no*
(5)
increase in sales. _____ this information became public, Vicary admitted
(6)
that he had lied about the results of his experiment.

---

[1]**subliminal:** below the level of what can be consciously seen

3 Read each sentence. If it describes an action that interrupts an ongoing one, write *I* (for interrupting). If it describes two actions in progress at the same time, write *S* (for same).

1. When Matt was studying marketing at a university, he was also working in a part-time job at a marketing consultant company. _*S*_

2. He spontaneously decided to do a quick research study on consumer behavior at a local shopping mall while he was taking a class on market research. _____

3. While he was doing this research, he made an interesting discovery. _____

4. While he was interviewing people, he noticed that they blinked their eyes more quickly if they liked a product. _____

5. Later, when he was explaining his research results in a meeting at his company, his employers weren't paying attention. _____

6. When Matt was driving home, he was thinking about how uninterested they were. _____

7. While he was getting out of his car, he suddenly had an idea. _____

8. All during dinner, while he was eating, he was writing down his idea. _____

9. While Matt was in his last semester at school, he started a global marketing company and made a lot of money. _____

4 Complete the sentences about people in the advertising and marketing departments at a company. Use the simple past or past progressive form of the verbs in parentheses.

1. While the people in the advertising department _*were discussing*_ (discuss) a new campaign, the marketing people _*had*_ (have) a brilliant idea.

2. When the boss _____ (hear) the marketing people's suggestion, he _____ (call) a meeting with the advertising team.

3. While the boss and the marketing team _____ (explain) their idea, the advertising people _____ (think) of ways to improve it.

4. The boss _____ (be) very pleased when he _____ (see) the two teams working together.

5. When the teams _____ (finish) the campaign, everyone _____ (need) a break.

6. So, as soon as the client _____ (approve) the campaign, the boss _____ (give) the two teams a week's vacation.

Used To and Would

1 Match the two parts of the sentences about how the marketing habits of a company have changed.

1. Until two years ago, my company __d__

2. The company didn't ____

3. They would ____

4. Last year, they hired a global director

   and ____

5. Now the company ____

a. use to have a global marketing director.

b. use the same ads in every country.

c. doesn't even use the same slogan in all

   markets.

~~d~~. used to spend very little on global marketing.

e. used different international campaigns.

That was a wise decision. Sales have been much better this year.

2 Complete the sentences about advertising in the past. Use the simple past, *used to*, or *would* with the verbs in parentheses. Sometimes more than one answer is possible.

1. My grandfather never _used to want_ (want) to pay any money for advertising for his small business. One year, he even _put up_ (put up) homemade signs around town to save money.

2. In those days, though, he _____ (support) my baseball team every year.

3. Every year, granddad _____ (pay) for baseball shirts that had the name of his company on the front.

4. We _____ (wear) the shirts in every game.

5. One of my teammates _____ (not like) wearing his shirt, however. He hated it.

6. He always _____ (try) to wear another T-shirt instead.

7. Once, he even _____ (refuse) to wear any shirt at all!

8. That day, his father _____ (tell) him that my grandfather was helping him have a chance to play baseball.

9. After that he _____ (wear) the shirt in every game without complaining.

10. My grandfather _____ (do) a lot of advertising that way.

Avoid Common Mistakes

1 Circle the mistakes.

1. When business **was** good and the marketing company **was making** a lot of money, it
         (a)   (b)
   (**used to giving**) many parties for its employees.
         (c)

2. Carlos **was attending** a business meeting when he **realized** he did not have the chart
            (a)   (b)
   he needed with him. He **asks** his secretary to get it for him.
                  (c)

3. Christina **worked** for a small company in Boston when **she received** an offer to work
          (a)   (b)
   for one of the largest marketing firms in the world. She **left** Boston to take the job.
                                     (c)

4. **Did you notice** all the product placements in the movie we just **see**? Many of them
      (a)   (b)
   seemed especially inappropriate to me.
     (c)

5. Our product **was selling** well in some markets, and our company **planning** on
           (a)   (b)
   introducing it to other markets as soon as it **was** possible.
                          (c)

6. When Robert **was working** for an international company in Italy, he **meets** his wife.
            (a)   (b)
   They **got married** in Rome.
       (c)

7. Omar and Hanan **were both studying** marketing while they **were raising** their two
                (a)   (b)
   young children. Hanan's mother **used to helping** them a lot.
                       (c)

8. Sylvia and Bob **worked** very hard for a big company when I first **met** them. Later they
           (a)   (b)
   decided to leave and start a small business that focused on protecting the environment.
     (c)

2 Find and correct eight more mistakes in this paragraph about a software design company.

> ABC Creative Software used to design software for the U.S. market only. They were
>
> doing very well and their business _∧*was* increasing every year. They would talking from time
>
> to time about "going global." Two years ago, the president of the company finally decides
>
> it was time to "go global." During the first year, they face many problems and global sales
>
> 5 are not good. Because they used to marketing their products to the United States only,
>
> they hired a consultant who helped them design better marketing strategies. Every week
>
> as the company developing, he would offer workshops in which he taught appropriate
>
> marketing strategies for different cultures. Soon sales were rising and the business doing
>
> very well. Soon after that, ABC Creative Software opened their first office in India. When
>
> 10 we called them recently, they celebrated this opening with a big party.

Self-Assessment

Circle the word or phrase that correctly completes each sentence.

1. _____ they were introducing their new product in Japan, they were spending a great deal of money on advertising.

   a. While   b. Once   c. Until

2. While the employees _____ the new product, they were doing market research.

   a. developing   b. were developed   c. were developing

3. _____ the customers read the terrible safety record of the new airline, they stopped using it.

   a. Before   b. Until   c. Once

4. Cooper, Brennan, and Schmidt started advertising as soon as it _____ legal for lawyers to advertise.

   a. is   b. was   c. was being

5. Electronic Widgets _____ a new store in Phoenix, AZ, in 2011.

   a. opened   b. was opening   c. used to open

6. When the big car company in town went out of business, many people _____ for new jobs, because they were expecting the company to close soon.

   a. looked   b. were already looking   c. used to look

7. When Peter was growing up, he _____ part-time jobs in order to make money to help out his family.

   a. would often getting   b. would often get   c. used to getting

8. When customers stopped buying as many cars as they _____ buy, the company decided that it needed a new image.

   a. used to   b. were using to   c. use to

9. My husband's first book, *How to Market Anything*, was published in 2009. _____ it arrived in bookstores, he began to travel from city to city to advertise the book.

   a. Until   b. After   c. Before

10. When John worked in the marketing department of Allied Software, he never _____ a day of work.

    a. was missing   b. misses   c. missed

11. While Marcia was discussing recent sales with her sales team, her supervisor called her and _____ her to come to her office immediately.

    a. would tell   b. told   c. was telling

12. _____ Emin could leave Istanbul for a business meeting in New York, he had to get a visa.

    a. After   b. Before   c. Until

13. That actor made a lot of money selling products on TV _____ he did something that made people dislike him.

    a. while   b. as soon as   c. until

14. That company _____ one of the most famous commercials of all time in 1997.

    a. created   b. was creating   c. used to create

15. Our company _____ pay much attention to our customers in South America, and we lost a lot of their business.

    a. didn't use to   b. used to   c. would

Present Perfect and Present Perfect Progressive

Present Perfect

1 Read the paragraph about Eric and his wife, Michelle. Then label the bold and underlined verbs *U* (unspecified time in the past), *C* (time that continues to the present), or *R* (recent action) according to the use of the present perfect.

    Eric **has just received** a really good job offer to manage a store in another town,

(1) *R*

Springfield. When Eric tells his wife, Michelle, about the job offer, she is pleased and

says, "Oh, that's wonderful. **I've wanted** to live in Springfield for so long." Eric says,

(2)

"Great. **I've been** worried about telling you all day. My boss **has discovered** that the

(3)   (4)

Springfield store isn't making much money, and he wants me to help change that.

He **has just offered** me a raise with the new job." "Well," Michelle says, "it's a great

(5)

opportunity. So far we **have been able to** save some money for the children's college

(6)

education, but we'll certainly need more." Michelle agrees that the job would be a good

move, and Eric decides to take the job.

2 Unscramble the sentences about Henry Chen's political career. Use the present perfect form of the verbs. Sometimes more than one answer is possible.

1. all his life / Henry Chen / an elected official / want / to be

   Henry Chen has wanted to be an elected official all his life.

2. for / he / live / 15 years / in Cupertino, California

3. he / for city council[1] four times / run / in the last several years

4. so far / not win / he / any election in his town

5. just / he / decide / to run for the school board[2]

---

[1]**city council:** a group of elected people who make or change the laws of a city | [2]**school board:** a group of people who make decisions about how to manage a school

6. not give up / Henry / still / on his dream

_____

7. never / he / become / discouraged

_____

3 Complete the sentences about a movie with *since* or *for*.

Our Success is a real success at the box office!

1. The movie has made $80 million *since* it opened.

2. It has been the most-watched movie _____ two months.

3. Attendance has gone up every week _____ the last three months.

4. Jason Prince, one of the stars, has not had a hit movie _____ several years.

5. Laura Noble, the other star, has been an actress _____ she was a teenager.

6. People have seen the two stars out together in public _____ the movie appeared in theaters.

JASON PRINCE   LAURA NOBLE

OUR SUCCESS

Present Perfect vs. Simple Past

1 Complete the conversation. Use the present perfect or simple past form of the verbs in parentheses. Use contractions when possible.

Tarek: _Have_ you _talked_ (talk) to Michael lately? What's he doing these days?
    (1)   (1)

Daisuke: I'm not sure. I know he _____ (finish) college two years ago, but I
                        (2)

_____ (not hear) anything about him since then.
        (3)

Tarek: What about Peng?

Daisuke: Oh, he _____ (move) to San José. He _____ (get) a
                (4)   (5)

new job a few months ago.

Tarek: _____ his kids _____ (start) school yet?
          (6)   (6)

Daisuke: I'm not sure. I _____ (not keep) in close touch with Peng
                    (7)

for a while. I know that he _____ (be) very successful in
                        (8)

his work, though.

2 Complete the paragraphs about a convict who escaped from prison. Use the present perfect or simple past form of the verbs in the box.

arrest	buy	give	receive	see
~~be~~	escape	not have	say	stop

Robert "Hoodie" Hudson _has been_ on the FBI's Most Wanted List

(1)

since he _____ from a prison in Texas 10 years ago. People

(2)

_____ him in several states since that time. FBI agents

(3)

_____ never _____ their search for him over the years,

(4)   (4)

but up until now they _____ any success.

(5)

Last week, however, the FBI _____ a call from a woman

(6)

who _____ she was Hudson's former girlfriend. She said,

(7)

"Hoodie _____ just _____ a plane ticket for Paris." She

(8)   (8)

_____ them his address in Austin, Texas. The FBI called the police in

(9)

Austin, who _____ Hudson the same day. Hudson is now back in prison.

(10)

Another success for law enforcement!

MOST WANTED

ROBERT "HOODIE" HUDSON

Present Perfect vs. Present Perfect Progressive

1 Write questions about famous people. Then answer the questions with the words in parentheses and *since* or *for*. Use the present perfect progressive.

1. How long / Bill and Melinda Gates / run / their foundation

Q: _How long have Bill and Melinda Gates been running their foundation?_

A: _They have been running it for about 20 years._ (about 20 years)

2. How long / Oprah Winfrey / work / in TV?

Q: _____

A: _____
(the 1970s)

3. How long / Venus and Serena Williams / play / tennis?

Q: _____

A: _____
(more than 20 years)

4. How long / Neil deGrasse Tyson / host / the TV show *NOVA scienceNOW*?

Q:_____

A:_____
    (2006)

5. How long / Lang Lang / play / the piano?

Q:_____

A:_____
    (he was three years old)

2 Complete the article about Emily's college preparations. Circle the correct verb forms. Sometimes more than one answer is possible.

Preparing for Success

Emily is a junior at the local high school. She

(**has planned / has been planning**) to go to college all her
(1)
life. She **hasn't decided / hasn't been deciding** yet whether
(2)
she wants to be a social worker or a medical researcher, but

she knows she wants to contribute something to the world

through her work.

Emily and her parents **have visited / have been visiting**
(3)
colleges lately. They **have seen / have been seeing** five schools so far, and they plan
(4)
to visit three more. Emily **has spent / has been spending** a lot of time recently on
(5)
her college applications. She **has written / has been writing** all of her essays for the
(6)
applications already. She **has asked / has been asking** several people to read the essays
(7)
for her. They **have all made / have all been making** suggestions, so Emily is now
(8)
rewriting her essays to improve them.

"All of us **have worked / have been working** day and night for several months on
(9)
getting Emily into a good school," say her parents. Her two older brothers and a sister

have graduated / have been graduating from college already, and now they have good
(10)
jobs. They **have had / have been having** a hard time realizing that their "baby sister" is
(11)
almost ready to go to college.

3 Complete the paragraphs about successful people. Use the present perfect or present perfect progressive form of the verbs in parentheses. Use each form at least once in each paragraph. Sometimes more than one answer is possible.

Michael *has been inventing* (invent) things since he was a child. This year he
(1)

_____ (already / invent) three new household gadgets.
(2)

When Mohamed arrived in London in 1995, he was already 34 years old.

Success _____ (not come) easily to him.
(3)

He _____ (have) to work very hard. Since 2005, though,
(4)

he _____ (run) one of the most successful employment
(5)

agencies in London.

Sarah _____ (be) a very successful hairdresser for years.
(6)

She decided to become a hairdresser when she was in middle school. Recently, she

_____ (think) about opening her own salon.
(7)

4 Complete each person's statement with the present perfect or present perfect progressive form of the verbs in parentheses. Use each form at least once in each statement. Sometimes more than one answer is possible.

Helen: I *have had* (have) two husbands. My first husband died in 1999 after our children
(1)

were grown. My second husband and I _____ (be)
(2)

married since 2003. He and I _____ (live) in Oakmont
(3)

Village for nine years. I _____ (love) both my husbands,
(4)

and I'm proud of my children. My life has been a big success!

Tomás: I was an accountant for a global corporation for many years. I retired in 2007 and

moved to Oakmont Village. I _____ (do) volunteer work
(5)

at the hospital every week since then. I _____ also _____ (take)
(6)   (6)

a lot of courses at the local community college over the years – Spanish,

nineteenth-century history, and even yoga. I think I've had a great life!

Isabel: I don't live in Oakmont Village. I'm here visiting my Brazilian friend

Raquel, who _____ (live) here since 2006. I
                        (7)

_____ (come) to see her here every summer since 2007.
          (8)

Raquel _____ (live) in several countries before this and
                (9)

_____ (have) several careers. She's a really interesting
          (10)

person.

Avoid Common Mistakes

1 Circle the mistakes.

1. Jordan **is living** in Rome since 2010. Her business **has been** very successful there, and
       (a)   (b)
   she **has been making** a lot of money lately.
            (c)

2. The news report about the winning design **have been** on TV every hour. They
                                                (a)
   have already interviewed everybody in the company, but they **haven't talked** to the
               (b)   (c)
   designers yet.

3. Daniel's parents **have bought** him a nice used car. He **has promised** to be a responsible
                        (a)   (b)
   driver, and he **has driving** carefully so far.
                      (c)

4. Since her daughter was born last year, my sister **is changing** her ideas about success.
                                                        (a)
   She **hasn't given up** her career or anything like that, but she **has been giving** much
              (b)   (c)
   more attention to her family and her personal life lately.

5. Greg **has been selling** three cars this week. He **has made** $4,000 in commissions since
              (a)   (b)
   Monday, and his boss **has been talking** about a possible promotion.
                              (c)

6. For several years, Theresa **has been growing** wonderful roses, which she **has selling** to
                                    (a)   (b)
   a local flower shop. Now, she **has decided** to retire and let her children run the business.
                                      (c)

7. Matthew and Amanda **are practicing** their Spanish every day for the past month.
                            (a)
   Amanda's company **has opened** a new office in Spain, and her boss **has offered** her the
                          (b)   (c)
   management position there.

8. **Have you been hearing** that the Swift Aircraft Company won a fifty-million-dollar
           (a)
   contract from that Chinese airline? They **have been trying** to get that contract for two
                                                (b)
   years! Now, they **have been celebrating** it for two days.
                          (c)

2 Find and correct eight more mistakes in the paragraphs about a businessman's retirement.

> Tom Wilson retired last year after a long, successful career in business. Since he
> retired, he has remodeled[1] the kitchen and has ~~been painting~~ *painted* the whole house. Now that
> it is finished, it looks new again! Tom and his wife, Barbara, has also taken a few golf
> lessons and have golfing once a week at the local golf course. Tom has a lot of extra time
> 5 and energy and have begun to do some of the cooking and cleaning. Barbara has had her
> own ways of doing things for years, and she has trying to find a nice way to tell Tom that
> he needs to find something else to keep him busy.
>
> Fortunately, the other day Tom ran into another retired businessman from his
> company who told him that he is doing volunteer work since last year at the Local
> 10 Business Association (LBA). He said he has been very happy and busy ever since he
> started. He told Tom that for the last few months he is helping a Vietnamese couple with
> their new business. Tom has already been calling the LBA twice today to volunteer, too.
> He has been having to leave a message both times, but when they call him back, he'll set
> up a day to begin. Now his retirement will be a real success!

[1]**remodel:** change to make better

Self-Assessment

Circle the word or phrase that correctly completes each sentence.

1. Manuel Chapple _____ great films for years, but he has never won an Academy Award.

   a. has made   b. made   c. makes

2. I've _____ that there is going to be a new film about the recent election this year.

   a. hear   b. heard   c. hearing

3. Kyle Desch _____ a successful campaign for governor a few years ago.

   a. ran   b. has run   c. have run

4. Soraya Samanta _____ about running for Congress recently.

   a. is thinking   b. has thinking   c. has been thinking

5. When she was 28 years old, Verónica _____ a successful career in the office of a university foundation to become a nurse.

   a. left   b. has left   c. leaves

6. How long _____ a manager now?

   a. is Paul being   b. has Paul being   c. has Paul been

7. Books about how to become a successful person _____ never _____ more popular.

   a. have ... been   b. has ... be   c. has ... been

8. *Think Yourself to Success* has been _____ thousands of copies a year for 10 years.

   a. sold   b. selling   c. sell

9. Has your cousin started her organization to defend ethnic minorities' rights _____ ? She used to say this was one of her main goals in life when we were in college.

   a. yet   b. since   c. ever

10. My uncle's store was very successful for a while, but recently sales _____ down.

    a. have been going   b. has gone   c. go

11. My father _____ to play tennis when he was 40. He's 60 now, and he still plays.

    a. learns   b. learned   c. has been learning

12. My friend Brian had two hit TV shows in the 1990s, but he has not had another hit show _____ several years.

    a. yet   b. in   c. since

13. My parents have been married for 50 years. They _____ their Golden Wedding Anniversary yesterday.

    a. have celebrated   b. have been celebrating   c. celebrated

14. The owner of our company is very happy that most of her employees _____ with the company for many years.

    a. are   b. has been   c. have been

15. Only three people _____ our department since 2011, and two of those people retired.

    a. leave   b. has left   c. have left

Past Perfect
and Past Perfect Progressive

Nature vs. Nurture

Past Perfect

1 Complete the conversation about a novel by the American author Mark Twain (1835–1910).
Use the past perfect form of the verbs in parentheses. Use contractions when possible.

A: Have you ever read *Pudd'nhead Wilson*, by Mark Twain?

It's a novel that says that environment is more important

than genetics.

B: No, I haven't read it. What's it about?

A: Well, the United States <u>*had abolished*</u> (abolish)
     (1)

slavery by 1894, when Twain wrote the novel, but people

_____ (not forget) slavery or the
     (2)

Civil War, which ended slavery.

B: Is it about slavery, then? Tell me about the story.

A: Well, it starts in 1830s Missouri. A beautiful young slave, who was named Roxy,

_____ (just / give) birth to a boy. The slave owner, Percy
     (3)

Driscoll, had an infant son, Tom, who _____ (be born) on the
     (4)

same day. The two babies looked similar. Because Roxy was only 1/16 African, she and her

son both looked white.

B: Is that important?

A: Yes. Roxy _____ (become) worried that Driscoll was going to
     (5)

sell her infant son, Chambers, to a slave owner in another state. She wanted to keep her

son near, so because the two babies looked alike, she decided to switch them. Her boy,

Chambers, became "Tom" and lived with the slave owner's family as their son. The slave

owner's son, Tom, became her son, "Chambers," and grew up as a slave. Because she

_____ (make) the switch, Roxy was able to watch her real son
     (6)

grow up near her.

B: This is starting to get confusing. I guess I need to remember that "Tom" was really

Chambers, and "Chambers" was really Tom. Right?

A: Right. Anyway, by 1850 or so, because of the switch that Roxy had made, "Tom"

_____ (grow up) as the son of a rich landowner and
(7)

_____ (become) a cruel, selfish person. Finally, he killed
(8)

someone. When they investigated the murder, everybody learned that "Tom"

_____ (commit) the crime. They also learned that Roxy
(9)

_____ (switch) the two boys.
(10)

B: What happened to "Chambers," the real Tom, who was the real son of the slave owner?

A: After they discovered the switch, he was freed. Unfortunately, he still felt like a slave,

though. He _____ (never / learn) to read and write, and he
(11)

talked like a slave, so he wasn't comfortable as a free, rich, white man.

2 Complete the sentences about Carol, a mother of twins, and her experience enrolling them
in school. Use the past perfect.

1. Carol / already have / several meetings with the principal.

   Before their first day of school, _Carol had already had several meetings with the principal_.

2. the mother / ask / to keep the twins together

   _____ , but the school put them in different classes.

3. they / always do / everything together

   That first day of school, the twins were very scared because _____ .

4. the twins / not make / any friends in class

   By the first week of school, the teachers noticed that _____ .

5. the twins / be / sick / for four days

   By the second week of school, _____ .

6. they / always get along / well

   Carol also noticed that the twins fought more. Before, _____ .

7. the twins' teachers / go / to the principal with their concerns

   Carol didn't know it, but _____ .

8. the teachers / put / them in the same class

   A few days later, when the twins arrived at school, _____ .

Past Perfect with Time Clauses

1 Complete the story about Dolly the sheep. Use *after*, *as soon as*, *before*, *by the time*, *until*, or *when*. Use each word at least once. Sometimes more than one answer is possible.

Many people had never even heard the word "clone"[1] <u>until</u>
(1)
they read about a sheep named Dolly. _____
(2)
newspapers around the world carried the story of how
scientists had successfully cloned Dolly, it seemed everybody
was talking about cloning. People talked about cloning as if
it were something completely new that had never happened
before. Actually, _____ scientists cloned Dolly,
(3)
there had already been a lot of small cloning successes in research laboratories. What
made Dolly different was that scientists had cloned her from an *adult* sheep cell, not an
embryonic[2] one.

_____ people learned about Dolly's cloning, they thought the idea was
(4)
very controversial. A debate began about whether cloning is a good thing to do or not.

_____ Dolly was born, most people had only heard about someone creating
(5)
life in a laboratory in books like *Frankenstein*, by Mary Shelley. _____ Dolly was
(6)
born, however, people had to think very hard about what cloning might mean in the future.

_____ Dolly died in 2003, she had only lived for six years, but
(7)
_____ she died, she had been a completely normal sheep, except for
(8)
having no father!

[1]**clone:** an exact genetic copy of a plant or animal created from a single cell | [2]**embryonic:** from an unborn baby

2 Write sentences about the twins Mariel and Marcie and their imaginary friend,[1] "Chippy."
Use the past perfect and simple past.

1. when / Mariel and Marcie / be / ready to start school / they / already / have / an
imaginary friend for two years

   When Mariel and Marcie were ready to start school, they had already
   had an imaginary friend for two years.

2. before / school / start / they / play / with Chippy all summer

   _____

   _____

[1]**imaginary friend:** an unreal person that some children create in their imagination and treat like a real person and friend

3. after / their parents / do / research on imaginary friends / they / decide / to talk to a psychologist

_____

4. before / their parents / make / an appointment with the psychologist / they / read a lot about the topic

_____

5. when / they / talk / to the psychologist / he / already / spend / 30 minutes with the twins

_____

6. by the time / they / leave / the psychologist's office / their parents / learn / that the twins were normal

_____

Past Perfect Progressive

1 Complete the sentences about a family with the past perfect progressive form of the verbs in parentheses. Use contractions when possible.

When Angela got home from shopping, . . .

1. Her sons Doug and Jason _had been watching_ (watch) TV for a couple of hours.

2. Her daughter, Alison, _____ (talk) on her cell phone for hours.

3. None of them _____ (work) on their homework.

4. The water outside _____ (run) since she left the house.

5. Her son Peter _____ (play) in the water and was completely covered with water and mud.

6. Her husband, Mark, _____ (pay) bills online.

7. The whole family _____ (not pay) attention to Brutus, the puppy.

8. Brutus _____ (chew) on a pair of expensive sneakers the whole time.

2 Complete the sentences about Oprah Winfrey's life and work. Circle the correct verbs. Sometimes more than one answer is possible.

1. Oprah Winfrey (had been living) / lived with her grandmother for the first six years of her life when her mother took her to live in Milwaukee.

2. After her mother **had been having / had had** difficulty with Oprah as a teenager, she sent her to live with her father in Tennessee.

3. Oprah became an honors student and an excellent public speaker after she **had been paying / had paid** more attention to her schoolwork for a while.

4. Oprah earned a full scholarship to attend Tennessee State University in Nashville after she **had been winning / had won** an oratory contest.

5. As an adult, in Chicago, Oprah **had been working / had worked** at a TV station for less than three years when they changed the name of her show to *The Oprah Winfrey Show* and they broadcast it nationally.

6. She had also co-starred in a miniseries while she **had been hosting / had hosted** *The Oprah Winfrey Show*.

7. After she **had been doing / had done** her TV show for about ten years, she decided to start Oprah's Book Club.

8. She **had been sharing / had shared** information about her own life with her fans for years before she found out in 2010 that she had a half-sister.

9. She **had been planning / had planned** to start her own TV network in 2009, but it didn't actually begin until January of 2011.

10. She **had been interviewing / had interviewed** people on television for over 30 years when she finally ended *The Oprah Winfrey Show*.

11. When *The Oprah Winfrey Show* ended, Oprah **had been appearing / had appeared** nine times on *Time* magazine's list of most influential people.

Avoid Common Mistakes

1 Circle the mistakes.

1. John's twin brother **went** to prison for the first time a couple of years ago. This wasn't a
   (a)
   surprise because he (got) into trouble with the police ever since he **was** a teenager.
   (b)   (c)

2. Krish was about two inches taller than his twin brother, Rajat. The doctors thought that
   this **was** because Rajat **has had** a severe illness when he **was** 10 years old.
   (a)   (b)   (c)

3. My twin sisters, Jennifer and Jessica, **have visited** several colleges before they **decided**
   (a)   (b)
   to apply to Washington State. They **considered** a lot of things, such as distance
   (c)
   and cost.

4. Before Diego and Ariel **got** married, they **have decided** to move to Ariel's hometown,
   <u>(a)</u>   <u>(b)</u>
   so they would be closer to her family. By the time they moved, Ariel **hadn't lived** in her
   <u>(c)</u>
   town for over a decade.

5. The twins Mark and Matt **had been graduating** from high school before their family
   <u>(a)</u>
   moved to California. Mark went with their parents, but Matt **chose** to go to a school on
   <u>(b)</u>   <u>(c)</u>
   the East Coast.

6. Before Dr. Wilson **began** his research, he **hadn't realized** that several other scientists
   <u>(a)</u>   <u>(b)</u>
   have already been studying the "nature vs. nurture" issue.
   <u>(c)</u>

7. Many years ago, I **saw** someone in the supermarket who I **haven't seen** in a couple of
   <u>(a)</u>   <u>(b)</u>
   months. When I called, "Yawen," and said hello, she told me she **wasn't** Yawen. She was
   <u>(c)</u>
   Yawen's twin sister, Ying.

8. The police said that they **had arrested** Nick because he **had attacked** a co-worker at
   <u>(a)</u>   <u>(b)</u>
   lunch. He explained that it was because he **had** a bad day.
   <u>(c)</u>

2 Find and correct eight more mistakes in the paragraph about searching for a twin.

When Mary's daughter was 10 years old, Mary told her a story about when she ~~has~~ *had*

been a young girl herself. She said that until she was about 10 years old, she has always

believed that she had a twin sister somewhere. Her parents had laughed and had said

that that was because she read too many stories about twins. Mary told her daughter

5 that one day, she has discovered a box of photos on the top shelf in a cupboard. She said

it looked as if it has been there a long time. The box contained an old photo of two little

girls who appeared to be about two years old. Mary said she immediately thought that

the photo was a picture of her and her missing "twin sister." She took it to her mother,

who began to cry. She told Mary that someone had been taking the photo of herself and

10 her twin sister 40 years before, but then a short time later, her sister had been dying in an

accident. All along Mary has thought there was a "missing twin," but now she knew it had

been being her mother's twin, not hers.

Self-Assessment

Circle the word or phrase that correctly completes each sentence.

1. My sister was shocked when she found out she was going to have twins. No one in our family _____ twins before.

   a. had been having   b. had had   c. had

2. In 2011, Mona tried to find her adoption records, but the adoption agency _____ .

   a. had already closed   b. has already been closing   c. has already closed

3. Scientists around the world _____ "nature versus nurture" for several years when they released their results.

   a. studied   b. has been studying   c. had been studying

4. Felicia's parents _____ her adoption papers since her birth, so she did not know she was adopted.

   a. hid   b. had hidden   c. have hidden

5. Seth and Eric _____ participants in several studies about twins before they began college.

   a. had been   b. had been being   c. have been

6. Until Matthew's parents both _____ , he hadn't known that he was adopted. He found his adoption papers in the attic of the house they left for him.

   a. died   b. have died   c. had been dying

7. The college did not hire Dr. Peters because he _____ had enough experience teaching.

   a. did not   b. have not   c. had not

8. When Joe finally paid off his student loans for his teaching degree, he _____ for ten years.

   a. had been teaching   b. has been teaching   c. is teaching

9. _____ Beth had learned that she had a twin sister, she spent years looking for her.

   a. Before   b. By the time   c. After

10. How many twins _____ Dr. Chang _____ before she published her article in *Genetics Today*?

    a. had . . . studied   b. has . . . studied   c. had . . . studying

11. Neither Julia nor her brother Jason had known they were adopted until one of their cousins _____ them when they were teenagers.

    a. had been telling   b. told   c. has told

12. Several years _____ by the time the scientists decided to start their experiments again.

    a. had passed   b. have passed   c. had been passing

13. The courthouse _____ by the time Brianna tried to research her family history, so she was not able to find the records she needed.

    a. had burned down   b. had burn down   c. has burned down

14. The research assistant had _____ played an important role in the twins study when Dr. Clark decided to add her name to the study as an author.

    a. before   b. as soon as   c. already

15. Paul _____ about opening a store just for twins until his wife told him that she thought it was a bad idea.

    a. had thinking   b. has been thinking   c. had been thinking

---

Be Going To, Present Progressive, and Simple Present for Future

1 Circle the best form of each verb to complete the conversation. Remember that the present progressive is used to express definite plans or arrangements and *be going to* is used to express general intentions and plans for the future.

John: Su Ho! I didn't know you were in town!

How's life in Hong Kong?

Su Ho: Hey, John! Life has been great over there. I'm

here in New York for business meetings for

a couple of weeks. I was going to call you.

John: Oh, will you be here next week?

I'm going to get / **I'm getting** married next
(1)

Saturday. Can you come to the wedding? **We're holding** / **We're going to hold** the
(2)

ceremony right here in the neighborhood. Do you think you can make it?

Su Ho: I'm not sure **I'm going to have** / **I'm having** time. **We're going to have** / **We're having**
(3)   (4)

several meetings next week in L.A., and we might have one on Saturday.

John: Please try to come. Marina's family **is flying** / **is going to fly** here tomorrow
(5)

morning. **They're all staying** / **They're all going to stay** at the Flamingo Hotel. We
(6)

could probably make a reservation for you there, too.

Su Ho: That would be great. I think **I'm probably going to come** / **I'm probably coming**.
(7)

I'll call you as soon as I know. I just have to check with my boss.

John: OK. **I'm going to make sure** / **I'm making sure** there's a place for you at the
(8)

hotel. Anyway, if you can't come, you can still watch the wedding. A friend of ours

is setting up / is going to set up a video feed[1] just before the ceremony, so you'll be
(9)
able to watch it on your laptop from wherever you are. Isn't technology great?

[1]**video feed:** a video of an event shown live on the Internet

2 Complete Fatih's e-mail to her friend Sanjay. Use *be going to*, the present progressive, or
the simple present with the verbs in parentheses. Remember to use the simple present for
scheduled events or timetables. Sometimes more than one answer is possible.

Hi, Sanjay,

I think you will finally have the opportunity to meet my boss, Dr. Simmons.

Dr. Simmons *is leaving* (leave) for Chicago tomorrow for the conference.
(1)
Everything is arranged. I _____ (take) him to the
(2)
airport at noon, and then I _____ (teach) his class
(3)
for him on Tuesday morning. You will be able to talk to Dr. Simmons at the

conference. The conference _____ (open) on Tuesday
(4)
at 10:00 a.m. Dr. Ramesh Gupta _____ (give) the
(5)
opening address,[1] and Dr. Simmons _____ (speak) in
(6)
the afternoon. There _____ (be) a "meet-and-greet"
(7)
party from 5:00–6:00, and then dinner _____ (start)
(8)
at 6:30. Dr. Simmons _____ (attend) the party, but I'm
(9)
not sure if he _____ (go) to the dinner. If you would like
(10)
to talk with him about your research, the meet-and-greet party is probably your

best opportunity. He _____ (fly) home the following
(11)
morning at 8:00 a.m.

Good luck,

Fatih

[1]**opening address:** the first speech at a conference, meeting, etc.

3 Write four sentences about things you plan or intend to do, or things that you don't plan
or intend to do. Use *be going to* or the present progressive. Use *not* when necessary. Write
sentences that are true for you.

1. _____

2. _____

3. _____

4. _____

Will and Be Going To

1 Complete the predictions in the blog with the correct form of the verbs in parentheses.
Use *be going to* when there is present evidence for the prediction and *will* when there is
no evidence.

How will technology change in the future?
What do you think?

Kate09: Small handheld computers and smartphones are becoming really
popular. People _aren't going to use_ (not use) desktop computers
(1)
at all in the future.

JackH: I really don't know. Maybe smartphones
_____ (get) smaller.
(2)

SMI960: Every year companies make products that are easier to use. In the
future, technology _____ (be) even
(3)
easier to use.

EvenTech: I really think that someone _____ (invent)
(4)
a way to send messages without typing or even speaking. It would
be great if you could just think of a message, and your phone would
send it.

ShellyB: People might wear smart clothing in the future, but in my opinion, this
_____ (not happen) anytime soon.
(5)

DrJHP: Right now a lot of doctors are using computers for patient information.
They even use computers in the exam room during appointments. In
the future, people _____ (not fill out)
(6)
forms on paper in doctors' offices.

2 Complete the conversations between different members of a family. Use *be going to* for predictions based on present evidence and *will* for requests, offers, promises, and decisions made at the time of speaking. Use contractions when possible.

A Husband: The remote control for the TV doesn't work. It

needs new batteries.

Wife: Hmm, I don't think we have any batteries at home.

Husband: I _'ll go_ (go) to the store and get some.
(1)

Wife: That's not necessary. I don't think that

I _____ (watch) any TV this evening. I feel like going out.
(2)

B Mother: Where's your homework? I _____ (check) it now if you'd like.
(3)

Son: I haven't finished it yet.

Mother: If you finish your homework early, I promise I _____ (let) you
(4)

watch a movie on our new 3D TV.

C Sister: _____ you please _____ (turn down) the music? I'm trying
(5)   (5)

to study!

Brother: Hmm. I _____ (do) that if you let me borrow your smartphone.
(6)

3 Write predictions about the future with information that is true for you. Write sentences with *will*. Then use *be going to* to write sentences that give evidence for the prediction.

Will

1. _____

2. _____

3. _____

Be Going To

4. _____

5. _____

6. _____

Future Progressive

1 Complete the story about a woman who is going to another country for an operation. Use the verbs in the box and the future progressive with *will* or *be going to*. Sometimes more than one answer is possible.

| give | pick | recover | spend | stay | take | ~~travel~~ | wait |

Medical Tourism[1] Is Growing

Helen Browning *will be traveling* OR *is going to be traveling* to Bangalore, India,
(1)
next week to have a heart operation. A car _____ her up
(2)
at the airport in Mumbai. It's going to take her directly to the hotel, where she

_____ the night. The next day she will fly from Mumbai to
(3)
Bangalore. A driver _____ for her there to take her to the
(4)
hospital. She _____ in the hospital that night.
(5)

In the morning, Helen has an appointment with Dr. Kothari, a specialist in heart surgery.

He _____ her a number of tests throughout the morning.
(6)
Her operation is scheduled for 9:00 a.m. the following day. After the operation, she

_____ in the hospital for about five days before they let her
(7)
go home. The excellent nursing staff at the hospital _____
(8)
very good care of her during all this time.

---

[1]**medical tourism:** the act of traveling to another location for health care, usually at a less expensive cost than in one's home
country

2 Complete the conversations about future plans. Use the verbs in parentheses. Conversation A is less formal (between sisters) and conversation B is more formal (a newspaper interview). Use the future progressive with *will* or *be going to*, depending on what is appropriate for each conversation.

A Mary's sister: What *are* you and John *going to be doing* (do) this summer?
(1)   (1)

Mary Lawson: John _____ (travel) for the next two months advertising
(2)

his new book, *The Future Is Coming*. He _____ (talk)
(3)

about his book on TV and in bookstores.

Mary's sister: _____ you _____ (travel) with him?
(4)   (4)

Mary Lawson: No, I _____ (work) on my own book, *The Future Is*
(5)

Already Here.

B   **Reporter:** What _____ you and Dr. Lawson _____ (do)
(6)   (6)

this summer?

Mary Lawson: Dr. Lawson _____ (travel) for the next two
(7)

months advertising his new book, *The Future is Coming.*

He _____ (talk) about his book on TV and
(8)

in bookstores.

Reporter: _____ you _____ (travel) with him?
(9)   (9)

Mary Lawson: No, I _____ (work) on my own book, *The Future Is*
(10)

Already Here.

Avoid Common Mistakes

1 Circle the mistakes.

1. I **told** everyone in the office not to text me for any reason on Saturday. I (will attend) my
   (a)   (b)
   sister's graduation in San Diego. I **will be** back in the office on Monday.
                                      (c)

2. Look at your train schedule. I think the train to Phoenix **leaves** at 1:00 or 2:00 p.m.
                                                                (a)
   I don't think any trains **will be leaving** earlier. I **going to wait** for you in the Phoenix
                            (b)   (c)
   station café.

3. When **do you think** the engineers **going to realize** that they **need** to improve the
         (a)   (b)   (c)
   latest tablet?

4. My company says in the company newsletter that it **will install** a totally wireless
                                                      (a)
   communication system during the summer next year. I **think** that **will be** a good thing.
                                                         (b)   (c)

5. TopStar Communications **is closing** early one day next week. The IT department
                          (a)
   going to do work all night, so you **will not be able** to access your accounts during that time.
   (b)   (c)

6. According to the schedule, the afternoon talks on new electronic devices **will begin**
                                                                             (a)
   at 2:00. We**'re not going to arrive** until 3:00. The presenters **will discuss** new devices
           (b)   (c)
   when we get there.

7. *Technology World* **is predicting** that by 2020 all of us **are going to be driving** electric
                      (a)   (b)
   cars. I **going to wait** until 2020 before I buy a new car.
           (c)

8. The workmen **will move** new workstations into the office for the next few hours.
               (a)
   Everyone **is going** home at lunch and **won't come back** until tomorrow.
            (b)   (c)

2 Find and correct the mistakes in the memo from a manager at a clothing business.

> *be wearing*
> The April issue of the magazine *Future Trends* says that in the year 2030, people will ~~wear~~ disposable clothing every day. If this prediction is correct, it going to have a big
>
> impact on our clothing business. We going to need to begin researching and developing
>
> ideas for creating clothing that people can wear once and then throw away.
>
> 5   Discussion of this topic starts tomorrow at our weekly idea meeting in Conference
>
> Room A. I'll travel next week in South Carolina to see our factories, and I am going to be
>
> discussing the same topic with plant managers while I am there.
>
>   There going to be a conference called "The Future of Fashion" in October of this year. I
>
> will attend that conference, and I hope to take at least one designer with me. I going to ask
>
> 10 all of you to vote at the beginning of September for the designer you think deserves to go.

Self-Assessment

Circle the word or phrase that correctly completes each sentence.

1. My sister thinks her son Billy _____ by the time he's three years old, because she plays the DVD called *Wake Up Your Child's Inner Genius* for him every day.

   a. is reading   b. is going to be reading   c. reads

2. There _____ always _____ unexpected consequences with the introduction of new technology.

   a. are . . . going to   b. will . . . be   c. will . . . being

3. Ming _____ a second home near the ocean if he sells his latest smartphone application for a good price.

   a. will buying   b. is going to buy   c. buys

4. Professor Dham predicts that a flying car _____ never _____ widely available at a reasonable price.

   a. is . . . being   b. is . . . going to be   c. will . . . being

5. That "Future Technology" conference sounds really interesting. I think I _____ to arrange my schedule so I can go with you.

   a. 'm going to be trying   b. 'll try   c. try

6. *Technology Buzz Magazine* says that a car that does not need anyone to drive it _____ available in 2040.

   a. is   b. is being   c. will be

7. My grandmother and her friends really enjoy using social networking sites. The retirement community my grandmother lives in _____ a wireless network very soon.

   a. going to install   b. installs   c. is going to be installing

8. My information technology class starts next week. It _____ on Tuesdays from 1:00 to 2:50.

   a. will meeting   b. are meeting   c. meets

9. CostLess Corporation has agreed that it _____ $20,000,000 to the Remedies Company in order to build three new offices.

   a. will pay   b. pays   c. going to pay

10. Ramesh won't be able to meet with us next Wednesday. He _____ presentations on how to store and analyze data every day for the whole week.

    a. will be giving   b. will give   c. gives

11. Reality Tech Company _____ some exciting new products. Anyone who wants to stay on the cutting edge of technology will like them all.

    a. will adding   b. going to add   c. will be adding

12. The technological changes we have been experiencing will definitely lead to important social changes. However, I don't think everyone _____ able to make the necessary personal changes.

    a. is being   b. going to be   c. will be

13. At 3:00 this Friday, my roommate Pierre _____ a presentation about how new technology has affected online education.

    a. give   b. going to give   c. is going to give

14. The Advisory Committee _____ its findings next Saturday in Deccan Hall.

    a. going to be presenting   b. is presenting   c. will presenting

15. I think the company _____ more people in the fall, but I'm not absolutely sure.

    a. is probably hiring   b. will probably be hiring   c. going to hire

Future Time Clauses, Future Perfect, and Future Perfect Progressive

Business Practices of the Future

Future Time Clauses

1 Complete the sentences about Meg, who is going to start an online company selling hats. Use future time clauses with the information in the chart. Sometimes more than one answer is possible.

1st Event	2nd Event
1. she / find a web designer	Meg / set up her website
2. the website / be ready	she / post pictures of her products
3. her customers / place a lot of orders	she / make more hats
4. she / receive a large order of hats	she / buy more materials
5. she / finish the hats	she / mail hats to customers
6. her business / make a profit	she / hire employees and an accountant
7. she / join an online networking site for entrepreneurs.[1]	the holiday season / arrive

1. _Meg will set up her website_ as soon as _she finds a web designer_ OR _she has_
   found a web designer   .

2. Once _____ ,
   _____ .

3. _____ not _____ until
   _____ .

4. As soon as _____ ,
   _____ .

5. _____ after
   _____ .

6. _____ not _____ until
   _____ .

7. Before _____ ,
   _____ .

---

[1]**entrepreneur:** someone who starts his or her own business, especially when this involves a new opportunity or risk

2 Complete the e-mail from a small business owner. Use *be going to* or the present perfect form of the verbs in parentheses.

Dear employees:

As you know, our small catering[1] business will expand in January. Please review this list of changes.

1. We will become partners with the company Dessert Delights. Once the companies _*have joined*_ (join) together, we _*are going to offer*_ (offer) their desserts along with our menu for all of our events.

2. We will use a cloud computing service. Once we _____ (install) the system, your work schedules _____ (be) online.

3. We are going paperless next year! We _____ (send) bills by e-mail as soon as the new year _____ (start).

4. We will stop using paper products to serve food. Workers _____ (wash) more dishes after events _____ (end).

5. These changes _____ (not happen) until the new year _____ (begin). There will be a meeting soon to discuss these changes.

---

[1]**cater:** provide food and drinks for special events

3 Complete the sentences about future events. Circle the correct form of the verbs.

1. Tina **is going to work** / **works** from home next year three days a week while her husband **is taking** / **will take** care of their children.

2. Next month, Charlotte and Sandra **are going to take / take** online orders for their business while they **are going to remodel / remodel** their store.

3. Denise and Andrew **are already planning / will already be planning** their new restaurant when the loan **comes / will come** through.

4. Dev **is meeting / will be meeting** with programmers about the computer problems when his business partner **arrives / is arriving** from Dubai.

5. Mia **is / is going to be** very careful with her money when her brand-new company **is starting / is going to be starting** up.

6. Next week, Tyrone **interviews / will be interviewing** salespeople while his business partner **is going to plan / is planning** the budget.

4 Complete the sentences about future events. Write sentences that are true for you.

1. When I finish this class, _____ .

2. While I am taking English classes, I _____ .

3. I _____ until I finish all of my English classes.

4. Once I _____ , I will _____ .

Future Perfect vs. Future Perfect Progressive

1 Complete the web article about a corporation's ideas for the future of business in 2020. Use the future perfect form of the verbs in parentheses.

- Many businesses _will have adopted_ (adopt) "green" practices. For example, more
  (1)
  offices _____ (become) very energy-efficient.
  (2)
- The cost of starting a small business _____ (decrease), and
  (3)
  more women _____ (start) their own businesses.
  (4)
- Global markets _____ (become) more interconnected.
  (5)
- Most companies _____ (hire) people to post comments on
  (6)
  social networking sites as a way to advertise their businesses.
- Many more workers _____ (take) jobs as contract employees
  (7)
  who work with different employers for certain periods of time.

2 Look at the chart with milestones[1] for the Gray & Taylor Company. Write sentences with *by* and the future perfect progressive.

Month	Who	Activity	Time
1. January	the company	operate	100 years
2. March	the director	work at the company	25 years
3. August	the sales reps	telecommute[2]	5 years
4. October	the employees	use software to set up meetings	3 years

1. _By January, the company will have been operating for 100 years._

2. _____

3. _____

4. _____

[1]**milestone:** important event | [2]**telecommute:** work for a company from home and communicate with the office by computer and telephone

3 Complete the article from a student alumni newsletter. Circle the correct verb forms.

What Are People from the Class of 2007 Doing Now?

Amanda Rogers will start her own business next year designing websites. By the time she

opens her business, she (**will have completed**) / **will have been completing** a degree in web
(1)

design, and she **will have designed** / **will have been designing** websites for five years. If you
(2)

need a good website designer, contact Amanda at arogers7@cambridge.org.

Rafael Martinez and *Anne Rosati* will have been married for seven years in June. Their bakery,

Artful Cakes, **will have created** / **will have been creating** amazing-looking cakes for five years by
(3)

that time. They **will have baked** / **will have been baking** more than 100,000 cakes by then! Look
(4)

for them at www.artfulcakes.cambridge.org, and order one for your next special event.

Keith Chen has been offered a job as a computer technician at a large corporation in Guadalajara,

Mexico. He **will have moved** / **will have been moving** to Mexico by the end of the summer. By then,
(5)

he **will have studied** / **will have been studying** Spanish at a local language school for at least a few
(6)

months. He is looking forward to the challenge of working in another country.

Avoid Common Mistakes

1 Circle the mistakes.

1. We will interview at least 10 candidates before we **hire** anyone. After I **interview** the
(a)   (b)
candidates, Jo will, too. Once we (**will make**) a decision, we will notify the candidates.
(c)

2. In May, Tanya **will have been studied** nursing for four years. When she graduates, she
(a)
will have been working at the clinic for two years. She **will probably get** a promotion.
(b)   (c)

3. We **will have completed** our business plan before the end of the week. By next month,
(a)
our financial advisor **have reviewed** it. By next May, we **will have opened** our business.
(b)   (c)

4. In June, Luke and his wife **will have worked** for Dr. Lee for four years. In July, he
(a)
have been a nurse for six years, and she **will have been working** as one for five years.
(b)   (c)

5. By 2025, people **will have been used** the Internet for over 45 years. Businesses
(a)
will have been using e-mail for over 30 years, and they **will have been working** with
(b)   (c)
computers for even longer.

6. John is going to update his office when he **returns** from vacation. When he **will create**

(a)
(b)
   new systems, he'll train the staff. They **will learn** the systems quickly.

(c)

7. By 2050, business **will have changed** dramatically. Technology **improved** a lot by then.

(a)
(b)
   People **will have invented** things we can't even imagine now.

(c)

8. My sister **finished** college by the time she is 21. I'm sure that, one year later, she

(a)
   will have gotten her first job, and she **will have moved** to her own apartment.

(b)
(c)

2 Find and correct eight more mistakes in the paragraph about a new business.

> Ana Ray will start a new child-care center after she ~~will get~~ *gets* a child-care license. Once she will get the license, she will remodel her home. By next fall, she have turned the first floor into a child-care center. By then, her family moved to the second floor. By the time the center will have opened, Ana will have been worked with children for 10 years. She will be working by herself when she first will open her business, but she may expand. By this time next year, she has decided whether an expansion is possible. She have made many contacts by then, so she will be able to find many customers.

Self-Assessment

Circle the word or phrase that correctly completes each sentence.

1. Tomas _____ his degree by the time I see him.

   a. completes   b. will have completed   c. is going to completed

2. Manuel is going to develop new software once he _____ his job.

   a. starts   b. will start   c. started

3. Employees _____ to work on the new computer system until it is thoroughly tested.

   a. won't start   b. will start   c. starts

4. The company _____ cloud computing as soon as the system is running.

   a. is going to use   b. use   c. has been using

5. Tracey will be installing the new computer system _____ the employees are on vacation.

   a. during   b. when   c. until

6. The employees are going to work from home _____ workers are remodeling the office.

    a. while   b. until   c. before

7. We'll be having a conference when the president _____ .

    a. arrived   b. will be arriving   c. arrives

8. By 2020, I _____ here for a decade.

    a. have worked   b. will work   c. will have worked

9. In January, we _____ the new security system for a year.

    a. will use   b. will have been used   c. will have been using

10. By the end of the week, how long will you _____ to get a new computer?

    a. wait   b. have been waiting   c. have been waited

11. Fei will have created a new website _____ the time her business opens.

    a. after   b. once   c. by

12. Keith _____ the manager of this office by this time next year.

    a. has become   b. becomes   c. will have become

13. I'll have _____ been working here for 10 years by the time the new computers are installed.

    a. as soon as   b. already   c. before

14. By this time next week, everyone _____ the news about the company moving.

    a. will have been hearing   b. will have heard   c. heard

15. How long _____ your computer when the new model comes out?

    a. will you have had   b. will you have been having   c. are you having

Social Modals

Learning How to Remember

Modals and Modal-like Expressions of Advice and Regret

1 Complete the conversation about advice for helping older people with memory and cognitive problems. Circle the correct modals or modal-like expressions.

Ada: This article has some great advice on how to help

older people with memory and cognitive problems.

Jia: What type of advice do they give?

Ada: Well, for instance, they say you (should)/ **had better**
(1)

be patient. It's not the person's fault if he or she can't

remember something.

Jia: That's a little obvious, isn't it?

Ada: They also say that you **ought / should** help the person
(2)

create a regular routine. A regular schedule helps a person be less confused.

Jia: Hmm. I'd never thought of that.

Ada: And you **'d better not / could** schedule difficult activities, like doctor's appointments,
(3)

in the afternoon.

Jia: Why not?

Ada: They say that people with memory and cognitive problems are often more anxious

later in the day.

Jia: Oh. I once heard that you **might not / could not** want to give them a lot of choices. It
(4)

seems that people with these problems deal better with fewer options. There's less to

have to think about and analyze that way.

Ada: Oh, that's interesting. They also say that you **should not / might not** have a lot of
(5)

noise in your home if the person lives with you. For example, if people are talking,

make sure the TV is off.

Jia: Uh-oh. I would have a hard time remembering to do that.

Ada: And another thing that experts say is that if the person's problems become more

serious, you **'d better / could not** get professional help from doctors and nurses. They
(6)

say you **should not / ought** deal with them on your own.
(7)

Jia: This is all good advice. It sounds as if the article was really worth reading. Can I

borrow it from you?

2 Complete the paragraph with advice about how to remember things. Use *could, had better,*
might, ought to, or *should*. Use negative forms when appropriate. Sometimes more than one
answer is possible. Use each modal at least once.

To help you remember information, you *should* divide it into small chunks. For
(1)

example, you _____ divide a phone number into several small parts.
(2)

You _____ remember it as 256-555-69-09 instead of 2565556909.
(3)

Another way to remember things is to associate something with the first letter of the

words you want to remember. For this method, you _____ write
(4)

down the words you want to remember. For example, if you are trying to remember your

classmates' names, write down their names and circle the first letter of each name. For

example, Ⓑethany, Ⓜarcos, Ⓢamantha, and so on. Then you _____
(5)

think of something that starts with each letter and associate it with the person. "Blue"

starts with "b," and Bethany has blue eyes. "Messy" starts with "m," and Marcos is messy.

"Smart" starts with "s," and Samantha is very smart. You _____ start
(6)

with a long list, or you will find the task too difficult. You _____
(7)

memorize a few names at a time, and then add a few more. Soon you'll discover that you

know everyone's names and you'll have a great new memorization trick!

3 Read the sentences about people who forgot or didn't do important things. Then give your opinion. Write one sentence with *should have* and one sentence with *shouldn't have*.

1. Jared forgot his teacher's name. He called her by the wrong name.

   He shouldn't have forgotten her name. He should have written it down.

2. Laura missed some English classes, so she didn't have any notes to study for the test. She didn't do well on her test.

   _____

3. Alison never writes down her homework assignments. Last night, she forgot to do her homework.

   _____

4. Charles had to give a speech for his class. He didn't practice it, and he couldn't remember everything he wanted to say.

   _____

Modals and Modal-like Expressions of Permission, Necessity, and Obligation

1 Complete the advertisement and list of rules for a memory experiment. Circle the correct modals or modal-like expressions.

Memory Tests at the Memory Lab

The Memory Lab is conducting research on how knowing more than one language affects memory. You **must** / **must not** meet the following requirements to participate.
(1)

- You **must / aren't supposed to** know two or more languages. One of the
(2)
languages **has to / doesn't have to** be English because the test is in English.
(3)
- You need to be able to speak, read, and write the second language, but you

  are allowed to / don't have to use it regularly. As long as you know it, it doesn't
(4)
matter how much you actually use it.

- For this test, you **are required to / must not** be at least 21 years old. We will not
(5)
accept participants under the age of 21.

Test Rules

Thank you for participating in the Memory Lab study. Please follow these test rules.

- You **were supposed to / must not** bring your ID with you. If the test administrator
(6)
has not asked for it yet, please show it to him or her before you take the test.

- You **were not required to / were not supposed to** bring food or drink into the test
(7)
area. If you have it with you, please throw it away now.

- You cannot talk to the other participants during the test. If the test administrator

finds you talking to anyone, you **will have to / aren't supposed to** leave the testing
(8)
area immediately.

- You **are required to / don't have to** stay for the entire time. If you finish the test early,
(9)
please wait until the hour is over. The test administrator will tell you when to leave.

---

2 A Look at the rules for things that students are allowed and not allowed to do during a test. Write sentences with *can*, *can't*, *may*, or *may not*. Sometimes more than one answer is possible.

Test Rules	Allowed	Not Allowed
1. Talk to your classmates.		✔
2. Talk to the teacher.	✔	
3. Ask the teacher for help with directions.	✔	
4. Use your notes.		✔
5. Use a dictionary.	✔	
6. Have your textbooks open.		✔

1. *You can't talk to your classmates.* OR *You may not talk to your classmates.*

2. _____

3. _____

4. _____

5. _____

6. _____

B Complete the conversation with the past form of the modals and modal-like expressions in parentheses. Use the test rules from A.

Drew: How was your test today, Kate?

Kate: It was really hard. We <u>*couldn't use*</u> (cannot / use) our
                                   (1)
      notes.

Drew: Really? _____ (can / you / use)
                         (2)
      a dictionary?

Kate: Yes. And we _____ (be allowed to / ask) the teacher
                             (3)
      for help with directions.

Drew: That's good. Hey, do you want to work on our science project now? Did you bring

      your laptop?

Kate: Oh, no. We _____ (not be allowed to / bring)
                           (4)
      laptops to class today. I left it at home.

Drew: Let's go to the library and use the computers there. By the way, where is your

      textbook? Did you forget to bring it with you?

Kate: Oh, we _____ (cannot / open) our textbooks during the
                        (5)
      test, so I left it in my car.

Drew: That was a good idea. Well, I'm sure you did well on the test.

Kate: I think so. But I got in trouble with Professor Jenkins, and I was really embarrassed.

      We _____ (not be allowed to / talk) during
                       (6)
      the test, and I asked Luis a question. I felt awful!

Drew: That's too bad.

Kate: I know . . . and I was only asking him what time it was!

Modals and Modal-like Expressions of Ability

1 Correct the mistakes in bold in the article about photographic memory.

is able to remember

Photographic memory occurs when a person **is able remember** a large amount of information accurately. Experts disagree on whether or not a person **can to have** a photographic memory. Some experts say it is extremely rare. They say that some children **are able to remembering** a lot of information. However, as adults, they **not able to do**

5　this. Other experts say that photographic memory does not exist.

Many people think that a photographic memory would be wonderful. Some researchers say this is not true. When people have photographic memory, they **are able store** a great deal of information, like a computer database. However, they might remember a lot of information that is not necessary for everyday life. Researchers

10　say that memory is only important when people **can used** it in their everyday lives. If people remember everything they see, read, and hear, they **will be not able to organize** the information in a useful way and recall it quickly when they need it. Also, sometimes people with photographic memory **can forget not** things they don't want to remember.

Some experts say that photographic memory is not something people are born with.

15　They believe that people who **can to remember** large amounts of information have to work hard so that they **can to do** this.

2 Write sentences with the present or past form of the modals and modal-like expressions.

1. Some people say that the composer Wolfgang Amadeus Mozart had a fantastic memory for music.

   They say he / can / play / very long and complex pieces of music from memory

   They say he could play very long and complex pieces of music from memory.

2. Most musicians playing Mozart's compositions nowadays don't have such extraordinary memory.

   However, they / be able to / memorize / his pieces by practicing a lot

   _____

3. Solomon Shereshevsky was a Russian journalist who never took notes during meetings.

   His editor / cannot / understand / how / Shereshevsky / be able to remember / everything he heard

   _____

4. Dr. Luria, who studied memory and the brain, gave Shereshevsky memory tests.

   The journalist / be able to / remember / a long list of numbers

   _____

5. Many students want to remember things as easily as Shereshevsky did.

   However, most students / not be able to / remember / information without studying

   _____

3 Complete the sentences about memory in the classroom. Use *could have* or *couldn't have* with the correct form of the verbs in parentheses.

1. Ms. Brooks *couldn't have remembered* (remember) all of her students' names. She had too many students.

2. Sandra _____ (learn) all of her classmates' names, but she didn't take the trouble to do it.

3. Elena _____ (get) a better score on the language test, but she was too nervous to remember what she had learned.

4. Jen and Mark _____ (give) their presentation today. Mark was sick and didn't come to class.

5. I _____ (read) Mozart's music diary like the teacher asked us to. I don't understand German!

6. I _____ (pass) the math test even though I spent weeks studying for it. I just don't understand the basic ideas.

Avoid Common Mistakes

1 Circle the mistakes.

1. You **shouldn't have stayed up** late studying the night before the test. You
(a)
(**should studied**) the week before the test. Good students **are supposed to know** such
(b)   (c)
basic study rules.

2. **I could studied** more last night, but I went to the movies. **I should have stayed** home!
(a)   (b)
I hope **I will be allowed** to retake the test if I don't do well on it.
(c)

3. My sister **could have been** badly hurt in the accident, but she had her seat belt on.
(a)
She **can't remember** the accident, but she didn't lose the rest of her memory.
(b)
I **supposed to be** with her that day, but I decided to stay home.
(c)

4. My friend **was able to get** her documentary movie about memory problems into a
(a)
festival. She **must not have paid** to enter it, but she **could have donated** money to the
(b)   (c)
film organization if she wanted to.

5. You **should have called** me for advice. You **should backed up** your computer. Now,
(a)   (b)
you **should buy** an external drive with a lot of memory or get a subscription to an
(c)
online backup site.

6. The test rules were OK. We **didn't have to worry** about spelling for the test because
(a)
we could use dictionaries. However, we **had to memorize** the important facts because
(b)
we couldn't use our books. But the best rule was that we **must not have stayed** for the
(c)
entire class if we finished the test early. It's so boring when you have to sit there waiting
for everybody to finish.

7. Mr. Lin **is supposed to give** us our final assignment today. We **supposed to work**
(a)   (b)
alone. We **aren't allowed to copy** information from other people.
(c)

8. You **should remembered** the teaching assistant's name. You **should have asked** a
(a)   (b)
classmate if you **couldn't remember** it.
(c)

2 Find and correct eight more mistakes in the article about an experiment on memory.

Cats and Memory: An Experiment

             was
   Anne Park ∧supposed to create an experiment to test the memories of cats. She

developed the following test. She put a block between a cat and a treat. The cat allowed

to get the treat, but the block was in the way. The first time the cat tried to get the treat, it

5 tripped over the block. The second time, it remembered the block was there and stepped

over it. Anne then played with the cat in another room and then repeated the experiment.

Each time she played with the cat a little bit longer. The cat remembered the block was

there for up to 10 minutes. After 10 minutes of play, the cat tripped over the block. Anne

was surprised. She thought the cat should remembered the block.

    Anne concluded that cats have memories of about 10 minutes. She must not have

10 turned in her results right away, so she decided to test her theory with more cats. She

borrowed 10 cats from a shelter and repeated the experiment. She allowed to keep the

cats for several days. The results were the same. Anne's boss thought the results were

successful, but she had some criticisms. She thought that Anne should tested even more

cats for her experiment. She also thought Anne's notes should included more details.

15   Anne supposed to return the cats to the shelter. She must not have found homes for

the cats, but she wanted to.

Self-Assessment

Circle the word or phrase that correctly completes each sentence.

1. You _____ try using flash cards to memorize new vocabulary. It really helped me.

   a. ought to   b. aren't allowed to   c. should have

2. Carlos _____ miss class. If he does, he might not pass.

   a. could have   b. shouldn't   c. has to

3. Erica _____ study for the test next week. She didn't do very well on the last test.

   a. had better   b. might not want to   c. is allowed to

4. You _____ memorize all of the vocabulary because we can use our books during the test.

   a. might not want to   b. might   c. are required to

5. Jake _____ be a part of the memory study because he's not old enough.

   a. may   b. is permitted to   c. can't

6. Are we _____ tell people about the research project?

   a. must   b. allowed to   c. can

7. Isabel _____ 100 questions for the English grammar test. She hopes she has time to finish them all.

   a. must   b. must answer   c. must have answered

8. Were you _____ your memory test yesterday morning?

   a. supposed to schedule   b. mustn't schedule   c. could have scheduled

9. The students _____ turn in their cell phones before they could take the test.

   a. must not   b. didn't have   c. had to

10. The doctor _____ give good advice on how to help patients who have problems concentrating or remembering things.

    a. shouldn't   b. could have   c. was able to

11. Cats have short-term memory, and they _____ remember most things for more than 10 minutes.

    a. aren't able to   b. mustn't   c. didn't have to

12. Fish _____ remember smells.

    a. are able to   b. are able   c. are allowed to

13. Elephants _____ survive in the wild because they have good memories.

    a. are required to   b. are permitted to   c. can

14. You _____ me the test was canceled. You knew I had missed the last class.

    a. won't tell   b. should have told   c. could tell

15. Jun _____ tested my photographic memory. I wouldn't let him.

    a. had to   b. should have   c. couldn't have

Modals of Probability:
Present, Future, and Past

Computers and Crime

Modals of Present Probability

1 Read the web article about creating strong passwords. Then read the passwords and the writer's opinion about them. Circle the correct modals to complete the sentences.

Stronger Passwords, Better Security

Follow these suggestions to create a strong password. A good password is one that is easy for you to remember but hard for someone else to guess.

- Make your password at least five characters long.
- Use a combination of letters and numbers.
- Don't use letters in alphabetical order, like ABCDE or MNOPQRS.
- Don't use your birth date or phone number as part of the password.
- You can use a foreign word, like your favorite color in German.

Password	Opinion
1. 569652	This password contains only numbers. Because there are no letters, it **shouldn't /(can't)/ may not** be a good password. The person definitely needs a different password.
2. Sept71992jb	This **couldn't / may not / shouldn't** be a good password. It contains a date, which could be the person's birthday. The person probably needs a different password.
3. blooppa	This password is a made-up word. That's fine, but it doesn't contain numbers. This **shouldn't / has to / might not** be a good password because it does not have numbers.
4. anaranjado629	This password contains a foreign word. It means "orange" in Spanish. The password also includes numbers. This **should / could / may** be a good password because it fits all of the suggestions.
5. 346b	This password is only four characters long. It is too short, so it **couldn't / might not / shouldn't** be a good password.
6. tyn80oh42	This password is over five characters long, it contains numbers and letters, and it is very difficult for someone to guess. It's perfect! This **has to / may / might** be a good password.
7. 49bcde1r	This password contains a combination of letters and numbers, but it also has some letters in alphabetical order. Still, it's probably OK. This **might / must / has to** be a good password.

2 Complete the conversation about hacking with the correct modals. Use the words in parentheses to help you. Sometimes more than one answer is possible.

Dana: Who do you think is hacking into our computer system?

Samir: I don't know. It <u>could / may / might</u> (unsure) be
₍₁₎

professional hackers. They steal credit card numbers

and other kinds of ID numbers because sometimes they

can make a lot of money from the stolen information.

Dana: Or it _____ (unsure) be an
₍₂₎

ex-employee. Some ex-employees who are angry with their old employer try to

make trouble for the company. Sometimes they delete information from computer

systems or even shut down the systems.

Samir: No way! It _____ (not possible) be an ex-employee. All our
₍₃₎

employees seem to be honest people. It _____ (a logical
₍₄₎

conclusion) be a professional hacker. It _____ (not possible)
₍₅₎

be anyone we know!

Dana: Well, it _____ (unsure) be someone from outside the
₍₆₎

company. But the company _____ (expectation based
₍₇₎

on evidence) be able to find out who did it pretty quickly. We have a good tech

department.

Samir: I know, the company _____ (a logical conclusion) have a way
₍₈₎

to see who is doing it.

Dana: You're right, and they _____ (a logical conclusion) know how
₍₉₎

to fix the problems it's causing. That's their job.

Modals of Future Probability

1 A Javier's company is paying for him to take classes for a certificate in computer security. He has written notes about the classes he plans to take. Read his notes. Then complete the sentences with modals of future probability and the verbs in parentheses. Use *will* (*not*) for strong certainty, *should* (*not*) for certainty, or *might* (*not*) for less certainty. Sometimes more than one answer is possible.

Required courses:	
IS 101: Information Security Basics	Definitely spring semester this year.
IS 201: Advanced Information Security	Probably fall semester this year or spring next year.
Optional courses (must take 3):	
IS 102: Internet Security Issues	Probably fall semester this year.
~~IS 202: Internet Privacy Issues~~	I've taken a course like this already.
IS 103: Forensic Computer Science	Possibly this summer. If not, next summer.
~~IS 104: Software Security~~	I prefer to take other courses.
IS 204: Network Security	Probably spring next year.

Javier _will take_ (take) classes to get a certificate in Information Systems Security.
(1)

His company _____ (pay) for all of the classes, so luckily he
(2)

_____ (not spend) any of his own money.
(3)

He probably _____ (not finish) the certificate this year because
(4)

he has to work at the same time. He _____ (get) it next year.
(5)

He _____ (take) the first required course this spring.
(6)

He _____ (not be) in school during the summer this year. After
(7)

he finishes IS 101, he _____ (know) whether he is going to take
(8)

IS 201 this fall semester. If he doesn't take it then, he _____ (be)
(9)

ready to take it next spring. He _____ (not take) the class IS 202
(10)

because he has already taken a similar course. He _____ (finish)
(11)

taking classes next year.

B Nicole works at the same company as Javier. Read her notes and write sentences about them. Use modals of future probability and the progressive form of the verbs. Sometimes more than one answer is possible.

> - Take summer classes from June–August, already registered and paid for
> - Finish degree in information security, must pass summer courses
> - Probably graduate January 4 if I take a fall class
> - Hope to get a promotion in January; not looking for a new job even if I don't get the promotion

1. take a vacation in June

    Nicole won't be taking a vacation in June.

2. take classes in the summer

    _____

3. take a class in the fall

    _____

4. graduate in January

    _____

5. get a promotion in January

    _____

6. look for a new job in January

    _____

2 Answer the questions with modals of future probability. Write sentences that are true for you.

1. Will you take classes to learn about computer security?

    _____

2. Will you change your e-mail password in the next month?

    _____

3. Will you pay your bills online this year?

    _____

4. Will you update the antivirus software of your computer in the next year?

    _____

5. Will you buy a new computer in the next year?

    _____

Modals of Past Probability

1 Circle the sentence in each pair that expresses greater certainty.

1. a. Scott must have read the book *Computers, Crime, and You.*

   b. Scott might have read the book *Computers, Crime, and You.*

2. a. He may not have learned anything from the book, though.

   b. He couldn't have learned anything from the book, though.

3. a. He must not have followed the tips in the book, because he had a problem with his computer.

   b. He might not have followed the tips in the book, because he had a problem with his computer.

4. a. Someone could have hacked into his computer last week.

   b. Someone must have hacked into his computer last week.

5. a. The problem could not have been very serious, because he fixed his computer pretty quickly.

   b. The problem might not have been very serious, because he fixed his computer pretty quickly.

6. a. Someone might have helped him, though.

   b. Someone must have helped him, though.

2 Read the information about different kinds of hackers. Then read the descriptions of people. Say what kind of hackers they probably were and guess what they did. Use *must have* if you are sure. Use *could have* or *may have* if you are not sure or if you are guessing. Sometimes more than one answer is possible.

Kinds of Computer Hackers

A black hat hacker: Someone who breaks into computer systems to steal information such as passwords, credit card numbers, and bank information.

A white hat hacker: Someone who breaks into a computer system legally. For example, a company might hire someone to hack into their computers to test their security system.

A phreaker: Someone who hacks into a telecommunications system. For example, a person may hack into a phone company's system so that he or she can send free text messages.

A hobby hacker: Someone who hacks into computers for fun. This person might try to change a program at home for himself or herself.

1. Dustin didn't like paying for text messages. On his latest phone bill, the phone company didn't charge him for any texts, even though he sent a lot of them.

   Dustin must have been a phreaker. He may have hacked into the phone

   company's system.

2. Silvia bought a lot of items using other people's money. She was arrested last week.

   _____

3. Debbie worked for a large computer company. The company paid her to break into their computers.

   _____

4. Claire borrowed a computer program from a friend. She didn't have the code to use it, but she hacked into it and copied it onto her computer.

   _____

5. Carl figured out a way that he could make free phone calls. The phone company caught him.

   _____

Avoid Common Mistakes

1 Circle the mistakes.

1. **Ben must working** for that new computer company. **He could work** in the IT
   (a)   (b)
   department, or **he might be developing** security software.
                   (c)

2. Limei **will give** a presentation at a conference on computer crimes next week. The
           (a)
   presentation **must be** about computer safety. She **will meet** with some of our clients.
                 (b)   (c)

3. Josh **might have lost** some important computer files. He **may have not backed up** all
        (a)   (b)
   of his files. A virus **could have gotten** into his system and destroyed them.
                          (c)

4. I **could finishing** my degree next year. I **may be getting** a promotion when I'm done. If
     (a)   (b)
   this happens, I **will be celebrating** with my family!
                    (c)

5. It **will be** difficult to prove Heather is the hacker. The company **won't say** it is her unless
        (a)   (b)
   they are certain. They **must not find out** if she did it because they probably will not find
                          (c)
   any proof.

6. People **might not getting** as much junk mail in the future. Computer programmers
           (a)
   may figure out how to stop junk mail. This **will help** solve problems with e-mail scams.
   (b)   (c)

7. More universities **may be offering** computer science degrees to their students in the
   (a)
   future. More IT people **might be learning** about computer security. Hopefully, hackers
   (b)
   must not be learning about it, too!
   (c)
8. **Anyone could have hacked** into your computer. **Could someone have guessed** your
   (a)   (b)
   password? **You might have not created** a good password.
   (c)

2 Find and correct eight more mistakes in the paragraphs about a woman's potential new job.

Erin's New Job?

               be

Erin might ∧ getting a job as a white hat hacker for a large computer company. She

may working with one or two other people to test the system. The hackers will try to find

weaknesses in the system. Erin thinks that she must enjoy this type of work if she gets

the job. She might starting the job in the next few weeks.

5   If Erin does get the job, she won't fixing the problems. Instead, she must be preparing

a report to the company. Someone else will fix the problems because Erin doesn't have

the experience to do that. She is upset that she cannot fix problems as well because she

would make more money. Unfortunately, she could have not gotten a degree in software

development because her college didn't offer software development classes. Instead, she

10 studied computer security systems.

      Erin might have not gotten other jobs she applied for, but that's OK. She's really

hopeful about her chances for this job. If she gets the job and does well, maybe she must

go back to school once she's making more money.

Self-Assessment

Circle the word or phrase that correctly completes each sentence.

1. Jim _____ be a computer hacker. He doesn't know anything about computers, and he
   would never do anything illegal.

   a. can't   b. must   c. might

2. _____ your password be too weak? Maybe that's why someone is getting into your e-mail.

   a. Will   b. Can't   c. Could

3. Mr. Simpson _____ having computer problems. He hasn't responded to my e-mail.

   a. might be   b. might   c. might not

4. It _____ be hard to find a good computer technician because many experienced people have applied.

   a. shouldn't   b. shouldn't have   c. should

5. You _____ have good security software already if your computer is not getting any viruses.

   a. shouldn't   b. can't   c. should

6. Mario _____ start his new job next Wednesday. He'll be working for Computer Plus.

   a. can't   b. will   c. must

7. Rina has to _____ home soon. She only works until 5:00 p.m.

   a. might come   b. be coming   c. coming

8. The new e-mail system _____ running by next week.

   a. must   b. may have   c. should be

9. Greg _____ likely get a degree in systems security. He has applied to the program.

   a. will   b. might   c. won't

10. Employees _____ expect new virus protection software. The company just updated the software last month.

    a. will   b. shouldn't   c. must

11. We probably _____ find out who the hacker is.

    a. won't   b. might   c. may

12. I _____ forgotten my password. It was my first name!

    a. could   b. may have   c. couldn't have

13. She _____ had a strong password. Someone hacked her e-mail.

    a. must have not   b. must not have   c. must not

14. The company _____ hired Peng. I'm not sure.

    a. can't have   b. might have   c. must have

15. You _____ gotten the e-mail about the computer problem. The tech department in the office sent it yesterday.

    a. have to   b. can't have   c. must have

Nouns

1 Rewrite the sentences about healthy lifestyles. Change the singular nouns in bold to plural nouns. Change the plural nouns in bold to singular nouns. Change the determiners to the words in parentheses. Change the verbs when necessary.

1. You should eat **a vegetable** every day. (three)

   You should eat three vegetables every day.

2. Some experts say it's healthy to get **10 hours** of exercise daily. (an)

   _____

3. Some people need to drink **a glass** of water every day. (six)

   _____

4. **Some diets** are too extreme. (that)

   _____

5. You should eat **one meal** a day. (three)

   _____

6. It's OK to have **several snacks** during the day. (a)

   _____

7. **All children** need to have a diet with enough calcium to build bones. (a)

   _____

8. It is healthy to add **a strawberry** to your cereal. (some)

   _____

2 Complete the paragraphs about fad diets. Circle the correct words.

A fad diet is a diet that is very popular and then disappears. In one fad diet, the dieter

ate mostly (cabbage) / cabbages and fruit. People on this diet cooked the cabbage with
        (1)

onion / onions, water / waters, and **salt / salts**. The **soup / soups** made from this recipe
  (2)   (3)   (4)   (5)

was bad-tasting. Often, those on this **diet / diets** did lose some **weight / weights**.
$\qquad$ (6) $\qquad\qquad$ (7)

However, this **loss / losses** mostly came from poor **nutrition / nutritions**. People would
$\qquad$ (8) $\qquad\qquad$ (9)

quickly gain back pounds once they stopped following the diet. It is certainly true that

vegetable / vegetables like cabbage are part of a healthy diet plan. However, on their
$\qquad$ (10)

own, they may not provide all the nutrients people need for good **health / healths**.
$\qquad$ (11)

Look at the websites of health organizations for good health **advice / advices**.
$\qquad$ (12)

For example, the American Heart Association website has quite a lot of very good

information / informations. It suggests that the most successful plan for most people
$\qquad$ (13)

is to eat less and to get regular **exercise / exercises**.
$\qquad$ (14)

3 Look at the chart. Write sentences about what you can and can't have on this diet. Make the count nouns plural.

	Diet Recommendations	
	Allowed	**Not Allowed**
1.	rice	potato
2.	chicken	beef
3.	fish	pasta
4.	nut	cookie
5.	bread	donut
6.	vegetable	fruit
7.	yogurt	egg
8.	tea	coffee

1. *You can have rice. You can't have potatoes.*

2. _____

3. _____

4. _____

5. _____

6. _____

7. _____

8. _____

4 Rewrite the sentences about health. Use your opinion and *the* + adjective for groups of people.

1. Elderly people need to exercise a lot.

   _____

2. Rich people don't always have a better diet.

   _____

3. Educated people know what kinds of food are healthy.

   _____

4. It can be hard for poor people to have healthy eating habits.

   _____

5. Sick people should exercise regularly.

   _____

Noncount Nouns as Count Nouns

1 Complete the sentences about people's likes and habits. Use the singular and plural forms of the words in parentheses. Use each form at least once in each item.

1. I always make *time* for yoga since it's my favorite way to exercise. I take a yoga class

   three *times* a week. (time)

2. I love _____ ! My favorite _____ are cheddar, Swiss, and

   feta. (cheese)

3. I don't like to eat red _____ , so I never eat _____ like beef

   or duck. (meat)

4. My favorite _____ are blueberries and raspberries, but I don't eat

   _____ very often. (fruit)

5. I drink _____ every morning. I prefer herbal _____ like

   chamomile and mint. (tea)

6. My favorite _____ are tomato _____ and cream of

   broccoli. (soup)

7. I like fast _____ a lot, but many of these _____ are unhealthy.

   (food)

8. I make my own _____ every morning because the _____ in

   stores have a lot of sugar added. (juice)

2 Complete the health plan Lisa's nutritionist wrote for her. Circle the correct measurement words.

Daily Diet and Exercise:

- Eat about six ounces of grains; at least half of the grains should be

  whole grains.

- Eat **three cups of** / **a slice of** vegetables and **two cups of** / **two drops of** fruit.
  (1)   (2)

- Have **a kind of** / **three cups of** milk or milk products.
  (3)

- Have about half **an article of** / **a pound of** meat.
  (4)

- Have only **five teaspoons of** / **a kind of** oil. Please notice that some foods,
  (5)

  like nuts and fish, already contain **a bit of** / **a slice of** natural oil.
  (6)

- Drink enough water for your individual needs. You don't have to drink

  eight pinches of / **eight glasses of** water.
  (7)

- Do **an hour of** / **a piece of** exercise every day.
  (8)

3 Complete Mark's diet and exercise plan with words in the boxes. Use measurement words and a noun for each item.

Measurement Words	
a few drops of	a pinch of
a game of	a slice of
a glass of	two cups of
a piece of	two quarts of

Nouns	
basketball	oil
bread	salt
corn	water
milk	watermelon

Grains: _A slice of bread_ and a 1/2 cup of brown rice
         (1)   (1)

Vegetables: A cup of spinach and _____ _____
                                      (2)   (2)

Fruit: _____ _____ and an orange
       (3)   (3)

Dairy: _____ _____ , some yogurt, and two pieces of cheese
       (4)   (4)

Meat: Grilled chicken with a little pepper and _____ _____
                                      (5)   (5)

Oil: _____ _____ used to grill the chicken
     (6)   (6)

Water: _____ _____
       (7)   (7)

Exercise: An hour of swimming and _____ _____
                      (8)   (8)

Modifying Nouns

1 Unscramble the sentences about a new gym.

1. big / new / a / gym / our town has

   Our town has a big new gym.

2. rectangular / pool / an / it has / enormous / swimming

   _____

3. exercise / modern / equipment / it has / great

   _____

4. big / weights / metal / there are / round

   _____

5. popular / the gym offers / classes / yoga

   _____

6. new / a / café / the gym has / wonderful / European

   _____

7. bowls of fruit / large / the café serves / delicious

   _____

8. healthy / there are also / in the café / Japanese / teas

   _____

2 Complete the conversation between a couple shopping for exercise equipment. Put the adjectives in parentheses in the correct order to complete the conversation. Add *and* when necessary.

Paul: This new resale shop is really big! We should be able to find the things we need

for our new exercise program. I'm going to look for *large plastic* (large / plastic)
(1)

dumbbells for exercising.

Steph: And I want to go to the clothing department first. I really need to buy a

_____ (cotton / new) T-shirt for exercising. . . .
(2)

Paul: Here are some T-shirts. That _____ (blue / white) T-shirt is
(3)

nice. Do you like it?

Steph: It's perfect. And look at that _____ (black / great) T-shirt
(4)

with the _____ (red / yellow) writing on it. It looks very
(5)

comfortable.

Paul: Hey, look at this _____ (green / purple / ugly) lamp! It's awful!
(6)

Steph: Wait! There's a _____ (antique / ceramic / lovely) vase next
(7)

to it. I wonder what it costs.

Paul: Hey, don't forget that we're just here for the exercise stuff. But let's go to that

_____ (coffee / French / great) shop on the corner
(8)

after we buy everything. We need and deserve a treat before we start our

_____ (new / exercise / fun) plan. We can have a slice
(9)

of their _____ (strawberry / delicious) tart.[1]
(10)

_____

¹tart: a pastry with a sweet filling and no top

Avoid Common Mistakes

1 Circle the mistakes.

1. **A 5-year-old** child should eat one and a half cups of vegetables a day.
   (a)
   An 11-year-old girl should eat two cups. (**A 25-years-old man**) should eat three cups.
   (b)   (c)

2. Livia ate **three slices of pizza** with **different vegetable** on it. She also drank
   (a)   (b)
   a glass of soda.
   (c)

3. The department of food services **recommend** eating healthy food. Nutritionists **write**
   (a)   (b)
   tips on healthy food. Their assistant **updates** the information once a month.
   (c)

4. That recipe calls for **two pepper**, **three onions**, and **one carrot**.
   (a)   (b)   (c)

5. The nutrition classes at that university **are** popular. The homework **is** difficult, but the
   (a)   (b)
   students in the program **is** very hardworking.
   (c)

6. I'm going to make lemon chicken today. I bought a **32-ounce bottle** of lemon juice, a
   (a)
   five-pounds chicken, and a **one-pound box** of butter for the recipe.
   (b)   (c)

7. My doctor told me that I should drink **eight glasses of waters** every day, try to get
   (a)
   an hour of exercise, and eat **several kinds of vegetables**.
   (b)   (c)

8. The farmer's market has a lot of fresh **fruit**. The **oranges** look good, but the **peach** don't.
   (a)   (b)   (c)

2 Find and correct eight more mistakes in the paragraphs about breakfast.

Kids Eat Breakfast

All ~~meal~~ *meals* are important, but breakfast is the most important meal of the day. It's sometimes hard to get children to eat breakfast. Here is a recipe that children love, and even a five-years-old child can make it! Put food colorings into a three-ounces glass of milk. Use your child's favorite color. Then give your child two slices of breads. Let your child paint a face on each slice with a clean paintbrush and the colored milk. Put the bread into the toaster. Remove it and add some butter. Most child love the fun faces!

Many recipes of this kind is on the KidsEat website. KidsEat is an organization that helps children eat better. The people at the organization is dedicated to improving children's eating habits. The recipe are easy to follow and delicious!

Self-Assessment

Circle the word or phrase that correctly completes each sentence.

1. There are several different kinds of _____ in the casserole.

   a. vegetable   b. vegetables   c. a vegetable

2. This recipe requires _____ tomatoes. Do we have any?

   a. the   b. three   c. a

3. I've concluded that _____ is the best exercise for me.

   a. a piece of yoga   b. the yoga   c. yoga

4. _____ is a major problem in the United States.

   a. Obesities   b. The obesity   c. Obesity

5. Do you think there should be food programs to help _____ ?

   a. the poors   b. the poor   c. poor

6. Jackie lost some weight and had to buy new _____ .

   a. pant   b. the pants   c. pants

7. _____ is really delicious.

   a. Italian cheese   b. Some kinds of Italian cheese   c. These Italian cheeses

8. Andrea and Mert had different _____ in the swimming class.

   a. the experience   b. experience   c. experiences

9. Two agencies of the United States Department of Agriculture _____ the Center for Nutrition Policy and Promotion and the Food and Nutrition Service.

   a. is   b. are   c. be

10. How many _____ do you have to move?

    a. furniture   b. pieces of furniture   c. pieces furniture

11. I only put a few _____ of milk in my coffee, and I never use refined sugar.

    a. grains   b. gallons   c. drops

12. My father gave me an _____ maker.

    a. ice-cream, Italian   b. Italian, ice-cream   c. Italian ice-cream

13. I use _____ bag when I shop instead of plastic bags.

    a. an old and cotton   b. an old cotton   c. a cotton old

14. My grandmother has a _____ cake recipe. I'm going to try to make it for the first time!

    a. traditional delicious   b. traditional and delicious   c. delicious traditional

15. Tammy has a _____ table in her kitchen.

    a. metal beautiful new   b. new metal beautiful   c. beautiful new metal

Articles and Quantifiers

Color

Indefinite Article, Definite Article, and No Article

1 Complete the conversation about choosing a color of paint for a room. Use *a / an* or *the.*

Diana: Hey, Lucas. I need your help. I want to paint _*a*_ room in my apartment, but
(1)

I don't know what color to paint it.

Lucas: What room is it?

Diana: It's _____ kitchen.
(2)

Lucas: How big is it?

Diana: It's _____ really small room. Why?
(3)

Lucas: Well, dark colors make _____ room look smaller, and light colors make
(4)

_____ room look bigger.
(5)

Diana: Really?

Lucas: Yes. Since _____ kitchen is small, you should definitely paint it _____ light
(6)   (7)

color. How about white?

Diana: I don't think so. _____ cupboards are white. I want to add some color.
(8)

Lucas: Well, how about _____ pastel yellow? _____ color yellow is cheerful, and it
(9)   (10)

will make your kitchen look bigger, too.

Diana: You know, that's a good idea.

2 Complete the sentences about colors with *the* or Ø for no article.

1. Pastels are _*Ø*_ pale colors. _*The*_ definition of *pastel* is a very pale or light color.

2. _____ colors _____ light pink, light yellow, and light blue are popular
   pastel colors.

3. Neon colors are very bright. Flashing signs often use _____ neon colors.

4. _____ pastel blue is a cheerful color that reminds people of _____ sky.

5. Metallic colors are shiny. They look like they have _____ metal in them.

6. Metallic colors such as silver are often used on _____ cars.

3 Complete the sentences about a color forecaster with *a / an*, *the*, or Ø for no article.

1. Lei is __*a*__ color forecaster.

2. _____ color forecaster predicts what colors will become popular in _____ future.

3. Lei is also _____ interior designer.

4. Lei does _____ research for her job. _____ research helps her determine popular colors.

5. Lei interviews _____ famous people about the best colors for homes.

6. Lei works for _____ company that designs and builds _____ homes.

7. If Lei is right about _____ popularity of a color, the homes built by her company are usually successful.

8. Lei says _____ color Berry Brown is going to become very popular.

9. Lei also thinks Grass Green will be _____ popular color this year.

Quantifiers

1 Look at the survey results about favorite colors. Then circle the correct quantifiers in the sentences.

We asked 200 people (100 men and 100 women) what their favorite colors are. Here are the results.

	Green	Blue	Brown	Black	Pink	Red	Purple	Orange
Men	24	37	0	19	0	14	2	4
Women	12	33	0	2	25	3	25	0

1. **A great deal of /(Many)/ No** men liked green, and **no / not much /(some)**women liked green.

2. **A few / A little / A lot of** men and women chose blue as their favorite color.

3. **A great deal of / All of / None of** the men and women picked brown.

4. **No / Quite a few / Most** men chose black, but **all / no / not many** women chose black.

5. **A lot of / All / No** women picked pink, but **quite a few / no / not a lot of** men picked it.

6. **A great deal of / All / Some** men chose red, but only **a lot of / a few / no** women chose it.

7. **Many / Not a lot of / Not much** women chose purple, but **a little / many / not a lot of** men chose purple.

8. **A few of / All of / Most of** the men picked orange, but **a few of / not many / none of** the women picked orange.

2 Complete the paragraphs about a famous painter. Use *a few, few, a little,* or *little.*

Few painters are as well known as Claude Monet. Monet was born in Paris, France, in
(1)
1840. At the beginning of his career, he had _____ success. In fact, he wasn't
(2)
famous, and he owed people money.

Monet painted some of his most important paintings in the 1870s. He painted

nature, but he only included _____ details. His style was called
(3)
impressionistic because it showed his impression of nature, not how things really looked.

_____ artists were painting like this at the time, so Monet's style looked
(4)
unusual and fresh. _____ people started to buy his paintings, and gradually
(5)
he was able to save _____ money. He bought a home at Giverny, northwest
(6)
of Paris, and made a garden. He painted the garden in many of his pictures.

In the 1880s and 1890s, he became successful financially and artistically. Today, there

are _____ people who haven't heard of Monet and his paintings.
(7)

3 Read the article about how animals see colors. Cross out *of* in the phrases in bold when it is
not correct.

> People can see **a lot of** colors, but exactly how many colors can they see? Experts do
> (1)
> not have an exact answer, but **some ~~of~~** experts say people see about 10 million colors.
> (2)
> The human eye can detect even **a little of** difference in color – for example, when a
> (3)
> color is just slightly darker or lighter than another color.
>
> **Not many of** animals see colors the way people do, but **some of** animals do.
> (4)   (5)
> **Not much of** research exists to show exactly how many colors animals see, but
> (6)
> scientists have been able to figure out **a lot of** things. Here are **a few of** fun facts:
>   (7)   (8)
> - Research shows that **quite a few of** insects are attracted to certain colors.
>   (9)
> - Bees can see **many of** shades of color that people cannot see.
>   (10)
> - **Some of** the research shows that dogs and cats only see **a few of** colors.
>   (11)   (12)
> - **Many of** scientists believe whales and dolphins are color blind. These animals can
>   (13)
>   see patterns in light, but **no of** colors.
>   (14)
> - **All of** scientists agree on one thing: **a great deal of** research still has to be done.
>   (15)   (16)

Avoid Common Mistakes

1 Circle the mistakes.

1. There are **much** trends with hair color. **Many of** the trends involve bright colors. My
   (a)   (b)
   sister has dyed her hair pink **many** times.
                                   (c)

2. **A lot of** my clothes are colorful, and **many of** them are bright colors, but **not much of**
   (a)   (b)   (c)
   them are neon.

3. Julie is **assistant** at a paint store, but she wants to be **a color forecaster**. She might get
   (a)   (b)
   a job in the field because her father knows **many people** in the paint business.
                                                (c)

4. **A lot of** people use digital cameras. **Not many** people take pictures in black and white,
   (a)   (b)
   but **alot of** people take pictures in color.
        (c)

5. **Not many of** my friends like the color pink. In addition, **a lot of** them don't like brown.
   (a)   (b)
   Much of them love black, though.
    (c)

6. Loretta is **photographer**, but she has been working part-time as **a photo researcher**
   (a)   (b)
   because she doesn't have **a lot of** work right now.
                             (c)

7. We don't have **much paint** left. There are **much places** we could buy more paint.
                   (a)   (b)
   Many of the places are downtown.
    (c)

8. You have **alot of** books. **Many of them** are about colors. Are you **a designer**?
             (a)   (b)   (c)

2 Find and correct seven more mistakes in the paragraphs about color forecasting.

Phil's Picks

Phil Wilson is ^*a*^ color forecaster. He looks at what colors will be popular in much

areas like fashion and interior design. Look at the colors he says will become popular.

- Orange is going to be very popular this year in clothing and in the home.

- Much earthy colors, like shades of brown, green, and blue, will be popular in home

5   decorating. However, these earthy colors aren't going to be popular in fashion.

- Wearing much colors at the same time will be fashionable. Wearing alot of colors

    together is going to be really popular with teenagers.

- Putting unusual colors together is also going to be a trend in fashion – for example,

    wearing red, orange, and purple together. These colors usually don't go together.

10   Mr. Wilson has been successful at picking alot of color trends in the past. Anna

Ramirez, who is interior designer, always considers Phil's advice. She says, "Last year, he

said that purple would be popular, and over 50 percent of my clients wanted purple in

their homes. This year, I'm going to be ready to use earthy colors and alot of orange!"

Self-Assessment

Circle the word or phrase that correctly completes each sentence.

1. I painted my room blue, because _____ color blue makes me feel calm.

    a. a   b. the   c. Ø

2. Night Blue is _____ only color of blue paint that the store has.

    a. a   b. the   c. Ø

3. _____ artist usually has a good sense of what colors look good together.

    a. An   b. The   c. Ø

4. Did you know that _____ people can be color blind?

    a. a   b. the   c. Ø

5. Please hand me _____ can of orange paint.

    a. some   b. the   c. Ø

6. _____ interior decorator is someone who designs the inside of a room.

   a. The   b. A   c. An

7. Let's take _____ class. _____ one about the history of color sounds interesting.

   a. a ... The   b. the ... A   c. a ... An

8. _____ research on color blindness was quoted in the student's report.

   a. Not many of   b. Not much   c. Not much of

9. Quite _____ the children said purple was their favorite color.

   a. a few of   b. a few   c. few

10. I know _____ the colors of the rainbow – red, orange, yellow, green, blue, indigo, and violet.

    a. many   b. none of   c. all of

11. Butterflies can see _____ colors. It is crucial for their survival.

    a. a lot   b. a lot of   c. much

12. Gabriel has _____ ability to see the difference between blue and green.

    a. no   b. none   c. not

13. Susan gets a great deal of _____ as a decorator.

    a. works   b. work   c. a work

14. Not many _____ are taking the black and white photography course.

    a. people   b. student   c. woman

15. There isn't any _____ online about the art classes.

    a. materials   b. schedules   c. information

Pronouns

Unusual Work Environments

Reflexive Pronouns

1 Complete the chart with the correct pronouns.

Subject Pronoun	Object Pronoun	Reflexive Pronoun
I	*me*	*myself*
you (singular)		
he		
	her	
it		
	us	
you (plural)		
they		

2 Look at the photos of two types of offices. Complete the sentences with reflexive pronouns.

an open-plan office

an enclosed private office

1. I can't see _myself_ working in an open-plan office because I can only work in calm, quiet places.

2. David imagines _____ working in an open-plan office because he likes to talk to co-workers.

3. Laura, do you tell _____ that you like working in an open-plan office?

4. Fang and Janet enjoy _____ in their open-plan office because they often need to work together and can sit nearby.

5. Sarah likes to talk to _____ , so she prefers working in an enclosed private office.

6. Marc and Sam, can you see _____ working in an open-plan office?

7. An open-plan office _____ can inspire people to be creative.

8. We would have to push _____ to stay focused in an open-plan office because there are more distractions.

3 Complete the article about a workplace. Use subject, object, and reflexive pronouns.

Imagine _yourself_ working in a creative job with a lot of benefits. Google is one
(1)
company that has many benefits. Google considers _____ a great place to
(2)
work, and others agree. It has made *Fortune* magazine's "Best 100 Companies to Work For"
in the United States for a number of years.

Google has many benefits for employees and their families. There are onsite fitness
centers for employees' use. The company also has child-care centers in many of its office
sites. Employees can bring their children to work, and _____ can also
(3)
bring their pets! However, when employees bring pets with _____ to work,
(4)
they have to take care of the pets _____ . There are many cafeterias onsite
(5)
at Google, and the meals are free. Employees can help _____ to food
(6)
throughout the day. Employees can also relax in the cafeterias. One Google employee says
that he enjoys _____ during lunch and that many creative ideas come out
(7)
of casual lunch conversations. One of the company's offices in California even has a car
wash, a dry cleaner's, a beauty salon, and a bike repair shop onsite.

Google employees call _____ "Googlers," and many of
(8)
_____ are happy with their jobs. One of the best things about working for
(9)
Google is that every Googler's opinion is important. When an employee has an idea, the
company listens to _____ or her.
(10)
Can you see _____ working at Google?
(11)

4 Complete the memo with reflexive pronouns. Add *by* when necessary. Sometimes more than one answer is possible.

To: All Employees

From: Paula Austin, Vice President

We have had an extremely successful year! I did not accomplish this _by myself_ . Every single employee
(1)
has helped us be successful, and you should all be

very proud of _____ .
(2)

I want to thank a few individual people for their hard work and contributions this year.

Sharon Mills started the Sales Reward Program _____ . Without any help,
(3)

she was able to create a program that will have a great impact on sales and will benefit

everyone. Adam Eckhart did the best in the Sales Reward Program. In spite of hurting

_____ this year while playing sports and missing a few weeks of work, he
(4)

still managed to get the most sales. Juan Garcia and Brianna Johnson created a plan to

improve employee productivity.[1] The two of them created it _____ – initially
(5)

without any help from anyone – and then asked for the other employees' comments and

suggestions. For every sales goal you reach, you get an hour off. Their idea is working

extremely well, and sales have increased even though people are taking more time off.

As we enter the next year, you might remind _____ of these examples and
(6)

contribute your own ideas.

Our president, Matt Davidson, _____ will be speaking to you next
(7)

week about our success, but I wanted to tell you the good news _____
(8)

before he came. I look forward to the next year being just as successful! Once again,

I'd like to thank you for your hard work and creative ideas, and ask you to congratulate

_____ for a job very well done.
(9)

---
[1]**productivity:** the rate at which a person does useful work

Pronouns with *Other/Another*

1 Look at the chart of employee benefits provided by some companies. Complete the sentences with *another*, *others*, *the other*, or *the others* and the correct form of *be*.

Company	Benefits
Company A	an on-site doctor, free health care
Company B	free counseling,[1] paid tuition,[2] free lunches
Company C	free health care, free laundry, free parking, free meals
Company D	an on-site gym, flexible hours, free health care
Company E	free child care, an on-site doctor, free health care
Company F	paid tuition, a company car, a laptop for home use, free lunches

1. At Company A, one benefit is an on-site doctor. *The other is* free health care.

2. At Company B, one benefit is free counseling. _____ paid tuition.

3. At Company C, one benefit is free health care. _____ free laundry and free parking.

4. At Company D, one benefit is an on-site gym. _____ flexible hours and free health care.

5. At Company E, one benefit is free child care. _____ an on-site doctor and free health care.

6. At Company F, one benefit is paid tuition. _____ a company car and free lunches.

---

[1] **counseling:** professional advice for personal or work problems | [2] **tuition:** money students pay for education

2 Complete the sentences about some company rules. Use *each other* or *others*.

1. Since there are two people in each office, you should respect *each other* .

2. So that you don't disturb your officemate, speak quietly to _____ when you're on the phone.

3. When you work with a partner on a project, please work cooperatively with

_____ .

4. In addition, you'll have weekly meetings with _____ in your group.

5. Please close the conference room door during meetings, so you don't disturb

_____ in the office.

3 Complete the conversation. Use *another*, *each other*, *one another*, or *the other*. Sometimes more than one answer is possible.

Ms. Smith: Hello, Morgan. Thank you for coming in. Since this is a new company, I want to get everyone's opinion on how things are going. What have you enjoyed the most about working here?

Morgan: I love working with my team – Janice, Paul, and Isabel. At first, I wasn't used to working with a team of people, but I've learned that if we communicate with <u>*each other* OR *one another*</u>, we get a lot done!
(1)

Ms. Smith: That's great. Your team works very well together. You obviously respect _____ . You and Janice seem to work exceptionally well
(2)

with _____ and with _____ teams in the
(3)   (4)

office.

Morgan: Thanks. Janice and I help _____ a lot. She's good
(5)

at technology, and Paul is good at design, so we all complement

_____ . Of course, it would be great if we could get
(6)

_____ person on our team to help us out when needed.
(7)

Ms. Smith: Well, Morgan, I'm very impressed with your work. I look forward to seeing

how your team continues to work with _____ . I'll look into
(8)

getting you _____ team member. Do you have any other
(9)

comments?

Morgan: I have two comments. The first is that we could really use _____
(10)

meeting room. _____ meeting rooms we have now are really
(11)

nice, but they're always occupied!

Ms. Smith: Yes, we know we need more meeting rooms, but right now we don't have the

money. Maybe in _____ year we can expand. What was
(12)

_____ comment you had?
(13)

Morgan: Oh, just that I love working here! Everyone is very nice.

Indefinite Pronouns

1 A Write the indefinite pronouns in the box in the correct columns in the chart.

anybody	everybody	nobody	somebody
anyone	everyone	no one	someone
anything	everything	nothing	something
anywhere	everywhere	nowhere	somewhere

People		Places	Things
anybody	_____	_____	_____
_____	_____	_____	_____
_____	_____	_____	_____
_____	_____	_____	_____

B Complete the article about unusual office spaces. Use the indefinite pronouns from A. Sometimes more than one answer is possible.

Google and Facebook both have unusual office spaces. The main office for Google is called the Googleplex. The Googleplex has several cubicles[1] with one side open. People can put almost _anything_ (1) they want in the cubicles, so each cubicle is unique. In one Google office there are many large fish tanks with beautiful fish in them. And there is also a bathtub in front of one of the tanks. _____ (2) in

the office can sit there at any time, look at the fish, and relax. In another area, there is an electronic map on one wall. People can see Google locations _____ (3) in the world on the map. There is also a room with a comfortable chair and a bright light. _____ (4) at all can sit in it if he or she needs a break. There is another room with video games in it. There is even a slide at the Googleplex. If you need a break at Google, there is always _____ (5) to do or _____ (6) to relax! _____ (7) working at the Googleplex enjoys the office.

[1]**cubicle:** a small divided space in an office

At Facebook, one conference room has a very long table and a long whiteboard all around the room. People can write _____ they (8) need to on the board during meetings. There are no cubicles at Facebook. The offices are open, and _____ works at tables. Some areas (9) have sofas, armchairs, and cushions on the floor so that people can have comfortable meetings. The environment is open, so _____ feels isolated. The office is unique. There is (10) _____ else like it! (11)

In fact, you won't find offices like either of these places _____ else in the (12) world!

2 Complete the questions with the correct indefinite pronouns. Use the word in parentheses. Then answer the questions with information that is true for you.

1. Do you know _anyone_ OR _anybody_ (any) who works in an unusual office?

   _____

2. If you could work _____ (any), where would you work?

   _____

3. Does _____ (every) in your family work?

   _____

4. Has a boss ever given you _____ (any) for your birthday?

   _____

5. Have you ever had _____ (no) to say at a meeting?

   _____

Avoid Common Mistakes

1 Circle the mistakes.

1. Everyone **gets** to request an office at work. Of course, everybody **want** the window
   (a)   (b)
   office. No one **likes** offices without windows.
   (c)

2. Luiza always gives **herself** enough time to finish projects. Brandon never gives **hisself**
   (a)   (b)
   enough time. Do you give **yourselves** enough time?
   (c)

3. Everyone **likes** to work with polite co-workers. No one **like** to work in a disorganized
   (a)   (b)
   office. Nothing **is** worse than working in an unpleasant environment.
   (c)

4. I have six co-workers in my group. We work well with **one another**. Felipe can be
   (a)
   difficult, but **the others** are easygoing. **Other** in the office wish they worked in my
   (b)   (c)
   group.

5. Everyone **enjoy** the new employee game room. Someone **is** always using it.
   (a)   (b)
   Unfortunately, no one ever **volunteers** to clean it.
   (c)

6. I interviewed for a job along with four **others**. One of the candidates seemed very
   (a)
   nervous, and he didn't seem to believe in **himself**. **The other** looked OK.
   (b)   (c)

7. Natalie wants to give **herself** a raise. The president **himself** told her that she couldn't do
   (a)   (b)
   this. Employees can't give **theirselves** raises or promotions.
   (c)

8. The two owners of the company worked with **each other** to give employees great
   (a)
   benefits. Some benefits are good for families, and **others** are good for individuals. Most
   (b)
   of the employees are happy with the benefits, but **other** think they could
   (c)
   be better.

2 Find and correct eight more mistakes in the paragraphs about unusual work environments.

Unique Work

Many companies have unusual work environments, but some are more unusual

others

than ~~other~~.

- At Green Mountain Coffee Roasters, employees can go take a class at the onsite

  meditation center. There, they can give theirselves some time to relax, and then

5 go back to work.

- At Chesapeake Energy Corp., employees can take scuba-diving classes. Some

  employees work toward a scuba-diving certification. Other just take the classes

  for fun.

- At Trupanion, a pet health insurance company, everybody receive free pet

10 insurance for their cat or dog.

- A number of companies offer a great benefit: everyone get a free lunch. FactSet

  Research is one company that does this, and other include Google, Facebook,

  and Netflix.

- Camden Property Trust gives a discount to employees who live in the buildings

15 the company owns. Anyone from the company pay 20 percent less in rent.

- Microsoft gives employees free grocery delivery. It also matches donations that

  anyone give to a charity. The founder of the company hisself gives a lot of money

  to charity.

Self-Assessment

Circle the word or phrase that correctly completes each sentence.

1. Do you push _____ hard at work when you have to complete an assignment?

   a. ourselves   b. yourself   c. himself

2. Nick and Ingrid brought their lunch to work with _____ .

   a. them   b. themselves   c. their

3. You don't need to help me. I can do it _____ .

   a. by myself   b. yourself   c. by himself

4. Lenny and Brad, don't be so hard on _____ . You're doing a great job.

   a. youself   b. yourself   c. yourselves

5. The ethnic diversity among employees is one of the two things I like about my office. _____ is the stress-free environment.

   a. Other   b. The other   c. The others

6. I've had five jobs in ten years. One was in an office. _____ was at a school.

   a. Another   b. Other   c. The other

7. I see one of your reports. Where did you put _____ ?

   a. one another   b. another   c. the others

8. The office environment is wonderful because everyone helps _____ .

   a. another   b. the other   c. one another

9. _____ is a better place to work than my office!

   a. No one   b. Nowhere   c. Nothing

10. Aya is _____ who likes to work in an open office.

    a. somebody   b. anybody   c. everybody

11. _____ can work in this office because it's too disorganized.

    a. Everybody   b. Nobody   c. Somebody

12. _____ with a design degree can apply for the job.

    a. Anything   b. Anywhere   c. Anyone

13. Can you trust _____ who works in your office?

    a. everything   b. everyone   c. everywhere

14. There is not another office as special as this one _____ in the world.

    a. nowhere   b. everywhere   c. anywhere

15. _____ in this workspace is modern, including the trendy desks and the lights.

    a. Everything   b. Something   c. Anything

Gerunds

Getting an Education

Gerunds as Subjects and Objects

1 Circle the gerunds in the article. Be careful not to circle the present progressive forms of verbs.

> | Elementary School | → | Middle School | → | High School |
> |---|---|---|---|---|
> | (ages 5–10) | | (ages 11–13) | | (ages 14–17) |

(Getting) an education is important to many young people in the United States. In fact,

young people must get an education. Starting school at age five, or even younger if they go

to preschool, is normal for most students. It depends on the state, but most students don't

finish studying until they are 17 or 18. Students go to elementary school, middle school

5 (sometimes called *junior high school*), and then high school.

Many high schools are offering classes that prepare students for college – for example,

advanced English, math, and science classes. These classes are called *college prep classes*.

However, not attending college is an option. Some students enjoy getting a job right out

of school. Taking vocational courses, such as car repair or computer skills, is an option for

10 high school students who are not planning to go to college.

2 Complete the statements about students' plans. Use the gerund form of the verbs in
parentheses.

John: I think *working* (work) after high school is important. I am considering
(1)

_____ (work) at a bank and _____ (move) to L.A.
(2)   (3)

Yawen: I have two years of high school left, but I've already taken advanced math

classes. _____ (plan) in advance is important, and I'm
(4)

considering _____ (become) an engineer.
(5)

Sebastian: I've always imagined _____ (become) a photographer.
(6)

_____ (pay) for the classes is expensive, but my parents have
(7)

been discussing _____ (help) me.
(8)

3 Complete the statements with information that is true for you. Use gerunds.

1. I've been discussing _____ with my family.

2. I'm considering _____ next year.

3. When I finish school, I wouldn't mind _____ .

4. I imagine myself _____ in five years.

5. I appreciate not _____ too much.

Gerunds After Prepositions and Fixed Expressions

1 Complete the blog entry. Use gerunds with the words in the box.

about / try	for / learn	~~in / make~~	on / use
at / educate	in / apply	of / have	

A Solution to My Issues with Education?

Readers of my blog know that I believe *in making* education available to everyone.
(1)
I dream _____ this happen in my lifetime. I recently heard about a
(2)
new university unlike any other – the University of the People. It started in 2009. The

best part is that it's free! Students are responsible _____ on their own.
(3)
Although students do not have to pay tuition, they do need to plan _____
(4)
a computer and an Internet connection. There are also some fees for the application

and for examinations. Anyone who is interested _____ to the University
(5)
of the People needs to be aware that the university is not accredited.[1] This is not

unusual for a new university, but it's important to know.

Will this educational experiment be successful _____ a large number
(6)
of people? I think it's a good idea, and I hope it's successful. Would you be excited

_____ this approach to education? Please join the online discussion.
(7)

_____
[1]accredited: officially approved

2 Read the conversation. Then answer the questions with gerunds as the objects of prepositions. Use the words in bold from the conversation to help you.

Nick: Hi, Ivan. Have you applied to any colleges yet?

Ivan: No, I haven't. I'm really worried.

Nick: About what?

Ivan: I don't know how I'm going to **pay for college**.

5 **Nick:** Well, you should **get financial aid**. You can learn about it from different websites.

Ivan: That's a good idea, but I don't like to **do searches on the Internet**. It's hard to find information.

Nick: It's not that hard. I can help you.

Ivan: That would be great. I usually **do everything by myself**. What colleges should

10   I apply to?

Nick: First, let's concentrate on one thing: how you'll **get money for school**.

Ivan: Good idea. I usually **think about too many things at the same time**.

       Then I give up.

Nick: Well, then I really have to **help you**. I insist! We'll start tomorrow.

15 **Ivan:** Great. Thanks, Nick. I'll **sign up for a computer** at the library.

Nick: Good. You take care of that and let me know when to meet you.

1. What is Ivan worried about?

   He's worried about paying for college.

2. What does Ivan need to learn about?

   _____

3. What does Ivan complain about?

   _____

4. What is Ivan used to doing?

   _____

5. What does Nick think Ivan should concentrate on?

   _____

6. What does Ivan admit to?

_____

7. What does Nick insist on?

_____

8. What will Ivan take care of?

_____

3 Complete the sentences with information that is true for you. Use gerunds.

1. I have a good reason for _____ .

2. In class, I have difficulty _____ .

3. I don't have trouble _____ .

4. After class, I spend time _____ .

5. I have an interest in _____ after I finish my
   English classes.

Gerunds After Nouns + *of*

1 Rewrite the sentences. Replace the words in bold with gerunds and the words in
parentheses.

1. Julia is **currently making** plans for college next year. (in the process of)

   Julia is in the process of making plans for college next year.

2. She understands **it is important to go** to college. (the importance of)

   _____

3. She thinks **the price to attend** college is expensive. (the cost of)

   _____

4. Julia is trying to figure out **how to pay** for college. (the best way of)

   _____

5. She's not sure **it's a good idea to take out** a student loan. (about the benefits of)

   _____

6. She is excited **that she may get** a grant. (about the possibility of)

   _____

2 Complete the paragraphs about student loans. Use the nouns in the box with the gerund form of the verbs in parentheses with *of*.

advantage	disadvantage	fear	~~habit~~	risk	way

You need to be careful when you take out a student loan.

Some students are in the _habit of using_ (use) loan money for
              (1)
things like rent and entertainment instead of books and tuition.

This _____ (spend) money
              (2)
can lead to problems for students. For example, there is the

_____ (not have) enough
              (3)
money for school expenses.

   One _____ (borrow) money with a student
              (4)
loan is that you usually don't have to pay it back until after you have graduated.

However, a _____ (get) a student loan is
              (5)
that once you graduate, you have to start paying back a lot of money. This can be

difficult for students who don't get a job after graduation. However, don't let the

_____ (pay) back a student loan stop you.
              (6)
You just need to be careful and be aware of the dangers.

Avoid Common Mistakes

1 Circle the mistakes.

1. My sister goes to college full time, and she is also responsible for (**clean**) the house,
                                                                          (a)

   cooking all the meals, and **taking** care of the children.
     (b)   (c)

2. **Eliminate** all fees for college students who need financial aid **is** one way to help
     (a)   (b)

   students. **Providing** free books is another way.
              (c)

3. Fixing computers **are** something Dan is good at. He plans on **working** for a large
                      (a)   (b)

   computer company one day. Finishing his degree **is** his goal right now.
                                                    (c)

4. Our visitors' main interest in **being** here today is not in **seeing** our whole campus.
   (a)   (b)

   Visit our new library is all they're really interested in.
   (c)

5. **Opening** an online university related to **saving** energy **are** sure to attract a lot of
   (a)   (b)   (c)

   attention.

6. Many of our international students are concerned about **not be** able to find good
   (a)

   housing. They worry about **finding** an inexpensive place to live or **having** to live too far
   (b)   (c)

   away from campus.

7. Jennifer works on her own in an office at a small university. She spends a lot of time

   interviewing all applicants and **filling out** a report on each one. **Have** an assistant
   (a)   (b)   (c)

   would help her a lot.

8. **Scheduling** classes at different times **benefits** students. Many students depend on
   (a)   (b)

   take classes early in the morning or at night, so they can work during the day.
   (c)

2 Find and correct nine more mistakes in the paragraph about Pam's studies and career.

Pam's Plans

       spending
After ~~spend~~ two years at a community college, Pam decided that she did not want to

transfer to the four-year university in her city. She thought about become a dog trainer

instead. She had dreamed of be a dog trainer since she was very young. She asked a

friend for advice. Her friend suggested volunteering at the Humane Society. Try to get a

5 job at a pet store to gain experience was another idea. Her friend also suggested reading

books and articles about dog training. After talking to her friend, Pam spent time online

searching for information. Check out websites were another good suggestion from her

friend. Interview veterinarians in the community also seemed like a good idea. Become a

dog trainer began to look more difficult than she had realized. She decided to transfer to

10 the university to study animal science and volunteer at the Humane Society in her spare

time. Concentrating on her studies are making her happy these days. Studying animal

science are the best decision she's ever made!

Self-Assessment

Circle the word or phrase that correctly completes each sentence.

1. Going to college _____ expensive in many places.

   a. being   b. are   c. is

2. Jorge imagines _____ a nurse some day.

   a. becoming   b. become   c. became

3. _____ long hours gives students more time to study.

   a. Not work   b. Not working   c. No working

4. Michelle _____ to a small college.

   a. is considering going   b. is considering go   c. considering going

5. Mona and Kelly discussed _____ to the same colleges.

   a. is applying   b. are applying   c. applying

6. I dislike _____ so much for my books. I don't have any money left for fun!

   a. paying   b. pay   c. am paying

7. Fixing computers _____ what Mike and Lucinda are good at.

   a. be   b. are   c. is

8. Are you _____ moving to a new city for school?

   a. afraid in   b. afraid of   c. afraid

9. Ji Sung learned about _____ financial aid on the Internet.

   a. getting   b. get   c. his getting

10. Mary wasted a lot of money _____ computer games instead of saving it for her books.

    a. buying   b. buy   c. bought

11. Did you have _____ concentrating in the advanced math class?

    a. time   b. money   c. trouble

12. I have a good _____ not finishing my homework.

    a. interest in   b. excuse for   c. in favor of

13. What is the benefit _____ to so many colleges?

   a. of apply   b. of applying   c. applying

14. Mike complained about _____ so many classes in one semester. He has seven classes.

   a. take   b. to take   c. taking

15. I am interested in _____ next year after I graduate. My parents prefer that I go to college.

   a. to work   b. work   c. working

Infinitives with Verbs

1 Complete the web article. Use the infinitive form of the verbs in the boxes.

| be | become | increase | not have | not waste | ~~show~~ | teach | work |

The Kay Morgan Agency, Inc.
Innovative Ways to Market Your Business

The Kay Morgan Agency hates it when good companies fail just because they don't market their products well. We would like _to show_ you how you can advertise your company in
(1)
new and innovative ways. In 2007, we attempted _____ with local
(2)
businesses that needed more creative marketing strategies. In the years since then, we have

offered _____ businesses how to make the best use of marketing
(3)
both here and around the country. We have expanded our business across North America, and

we hope _____ a global company in the future.
(4)

The Kay Morgan Agency works with companies of all sizes. Sometimes large companies

seem _____ conservative in their advertising strategies,
(5)
so we help them be more creative. On the other hand, small business owners tend

_____ the tools they need for advertising. It doesn't matter if
(6)
you're a large or small company. When you hire The Kay Morgan Agency, we'll manage

_____ your sales in two months. Contact us today and find out what
(7)
we can do to help you. We promise _____ your time.
(8)

2 Complete the article about innovative marketing. Circle the correct form of the verbs. Sometimes more than one answer is possible.

With all of the innovative ways to market products, word-of-mouth can still be a very effective way to advertise. Take Jim Harris as an example. He was starting a painting business. He wanted (**to get**)/ **him to get** as many customers as possible, but he didn't
(1)
have a lot of money for advertising. He offered **to paint / her to paint** the office of a
(2)
veterinarian[1] in his town. Dr. Lee, the veterinarian, agreed. She wanted **to put / him to put**
(3)
pictures of animals on the walls, so he chose **to create / her to create** a large painting
(4)
with various pets, such as cats, dogs, turtles, and birds. It filled an entire wall.

When he was finished painting, Jim asked **to leave / him to leave** some of his business
(5)
cards at the front desk. Leaving his cards helped **to advertise / them to advertise** his
(6)
business. Many people who came into the office commented on the painting, and Dr. Lee
asked if they would like **to take / them to take** one of Jim's business cards. Many people
(7)
took one, and some of them asked **to paint / Jim to paint** their homes. Today, Jim has a
(8)
successful business that started by word-of-mouth.

---
[1]**veterinarian:** an animal doctor

3 Unscramble the sentences. Use the simple past form of one verb and the infinitive form of the other verb.

1. help / the Linden advertising agency / Marcelo Garcia / his clothing business / market

   The Linden advertising agency helped Marcelo Garcia to market his

   clothing business.

2. spend / him / Ms. Linden / more money on advertising / tell

   _____

3. creative advertising methods / urge / him / she / use

   _____

4. her / give / him / ask / he / some ideas

   _____

5. put / choose / Marcelo / ads in teen magazines

   _____

6. young consumers / buy / the advertisements / Marcelo's clothing / persuade

   _____

Infinitives vs. Gerunds

1 A Phone Globe asked customers to complete an online service survey. Write sentences about Nicole's survey answers. Use the underlined verbs with infinitives or gerunds.

We hope our customers at Phone Globe are happy with their cell phones. Please take a few minutes to fill out this survey and help us improve our service.

Click on the word that best describes how you feel about doing these things on your cell phone:

	Love	Like	Don't like	Hate
1. Sending text messages	◉	○	○	○
2. Calling friends	○	○	○	◉
3. Checking e-mail	○	◉	○	○
4. Using the Internet	○	○	◉	○

Click on the choice that you <u>prefer</u>:

5. Taking pictures with a phone	○
Taking pictures with a camera	◉
6. Checking e-mail on your phone	◉
Checking e-mail on your computer	○

Click on the answer to the questions:

	Last year	More than a year ago
7. When did you <u>begin</u> using our phone service?	◉	○

	Yes	No
8. Will you <u>continue</u> using our phone service?	◉	○

1. (infinitive)   _Nicole loves to send text messages on her cell phone._

2. (gerund)   _____

3. (infinitive)   _____

4. (gerund)   _____

5. (infinitive)   _____

6. (gerund)   _____

7. (infinitive)   _____

8. (gerund)   _____

B Answer the questions with your own opinions. If the question uses a gerund, answer with an infinitive. If the question uses an infinitive, answer with a gerund. Write sentences that are true for you.

1. What do you think about sending text messages?

_____

2. Do you prefer to call friends or to send them text messages?

_____

3. Do you like to use the Internet on your phone?

_____

4. Do you prefer taking pictures with a phone or with a camera?

_____

5. Do you prefer to check e-mail on your phone or on a computer?

_____

2 Complete the paragraph. Circle the correct gerunds or infinitives.

Last night, Dan stopped **to read /(reading)** his marketing homework at 8:00. He wasn't
(1)
finished, but he planned to finish it at lunch today. Unfortunately, he didn't remember

to put / putting the article in his book bag last night. At lunch, he realized that he had
(2)
forgotten **to bring / bringing** the article to school. He remembered **to leave / leaving** it
(3)   (4)
on his desk at home. He regretted **not to have / not having** the article with him so that
(5)
he could finish reading it. Before class, he stopped **to discuss / discussing** his problem
(6)
with Sally. He tried **to get / getting** her to tell him about the article, but she wouldn't do
(7)
it. In fact, she stopped **to discuss / discussing** the problem completely, and she walked
(8)
away. In class, Dan tried **to pretend / pretending** that he had read the article. It worked
(9)
for a few minutes, but when the teacher called on him to answer a question about the end

of the article, he admitted that he hadn't finished it. She replied, "I regret **to tell / telling**
(10)
you that you'll have to stay after class to talk with me about not doing your homework."

Infinitives After Adjectives and Nouns

1 Complete the web article with the pairs of phrases and words in the box. Use the infinitive form of the second verb in each pair. Sometimes more than one answer is possible.

be easy / do	not be afraid / give away	not be necessary / shock
be likely / buy	not be difficult / post	will be amazed / discover
be lucky / become	~~not be embarrassed / let~~	will be surprised / find
be ready / hear		

Do you play music in a band? Is your band tired of playing to small audiences?

Here are some tips on how to advertise your band.

- _Do not be embarrassed to let_ others hear and see you on their computers.
  (1)

  It _____ a video of your band online.
  (2)

  You _____ how many people go
  (3)

  to see a band after hearing them online. They hear one song, and they

  _____ more.
  (4)

- _____ some music for free. You
  (5)

  _____ that sales often increase when
  (6)

  you give away free music. Let listeners download one song for free, and they

  _____ more songs.
  (7)

- Many artists today think they have to do something dramatic to get people to listen

  to their work, but it _____ your audience to
  (8)

  get attention. It _____ what everyone else
  (9)

  is doing, but you'll be more successful if you do your own thing.

- Remember that bands _____ well known.
  (10)

  Be patient and have fun while you are trying to be successful!

2 Complete the sentences about Marc's new invention with the words in the box. Use the infinitive form of the verbs. Then check (✓) *Agree* or *Disagree* to say whether or not you agree with the statements.

> ### It's a hat. It's sunglasses!
> Never lose your sunglasses again!
> Buy the Hat-for-Eyes today for only $10.
> The first 100 people to order
> get one free!

ability / change	chance / sell	~~decision / hire~~	time / buy	way / get

		Agree	Disagree
1. Marc made the _decision to hire_ a marketing expert.		____	____
2. His ad is one _____ a lot of attention.		____	____
3. He'll have the _____ his product to a lot of people.		____	____
4. His product has the _____ lives.		____	____
5. It's _____ a Hat-for-Eyes!		____	____

Avoid Common Mistakes

1 Circle the mistakes.

1. Lori **wants to start** a company. She ⟨**wants that people buy**⟩ her product. She really
   (a)   (b)
   needs to get marketing advice.
   (c)

2. **Jeff forgot to read** the marketing report, so **he decided to not finish** his homework.
   (a)   (b)
   He doesn't seem to care much about his grades.
   (c)

3. Luisa **loves to seeing** new bands. She **looks forward to listening** to new music online.
   (a)   (b)
   Sometimes, she **decides to buy** the music.
   (c)

4. It's **easy to market** new products nowadays, but it's **important to find** the best way.
   (a)   (b)
   A very effective **way for advertise** to young customers is on social networking sites.
   (c)

5. Alex **doesn't admit to make** mistakes very often. She **can't stand making** mistakes at
   (a)   (b)
   work. She **confessed to making** a mistake with the marketing plan.
   (c)

6. Larry **planned to not buy** a computer for a long time. An advertisement that he saw
   (a)
   persuaded him to get a new computer. He **promised not to fall** for ads in the future.
   (b)   (c)

7. I **want to believe** what the company says about this product, but I'm really
   (a)
   worried that it won't work. I **want that the company give** my money back if it
   (b)   (c)
   doesn't work.

8. I **hope to take** a marketing class next year. I **plan for study** international marketing.
   (a)   (b)
   I **love learning** about ways people market products in other places.
   (c)

2 Find and correct the mistakes in the article about false advertising.

False Advertising

False advertising is giving untrue information about a product. Some stores use false

advertising because they want ~~that~~ you ^to^ come inside. Here are some common forms of

false advertising that stores use to persuade you to buying their products:

- Some companies use pictures that make their products look better than they are.

5   Maybe you see a picture of a great computer online. When you get to the store, the

   computer looks very different. The salespeople then offer you another, more expensive,

   computer.

- Some stores advertise great sales. You look forward to buy the product you see, but

   when you get to the store, the item you want for buy is gone. Once you're in the store,

10   salespeople urge you to not leave without buying something.

- Some advertisements or salespeople say a product can do something that it can't do.

   They convince that you get it, and then you're disappointed when you get home.

   Be careful of false advertising when you shop. We don't want that you be disappointed.

Self-Assessment

Circle the word or phrase that correctly completes each sentence.

1. The company's advertisements tend _____ incorrect.

   a. be   b. to be   c. being

2. I hope _____ my marketing homework before midnight.

   a. finish   b. to finish   c. finishing

3. The marketing director promised _____ anyone with the new ads.

    a. to not shock   b. not to shocking   c. not to shock

4. Did you want to buy a new computer, or did the salesperson convince _____ ?

    a. you get it   b. to get it   c. you to get it

5. I chose _____ a new cell phone. The ad made it look great!

    a. to buy   b. it to buy   c. me to buy

6. Did you ask _____ the report today? I don't think he's done yet.

    a. to finish   b. Dustin to finish   c. Dustin finishing

7. The company began _____ a lot of sales after it advertised online.

    a. to get   b. get   c. to getting

8. Paul can't stand _____ advertisements in his e-mail.

    a. receive   b. receiving   c. to not receive

9. We stopped _____ our product because it wasn't good for the environment.

    a. to sell   b. selling   c. sell

10. Don't forget _____ at products carefully before you buy them. Sometimes companies use false advertising.

    a. to look   b. looking   c. look

11. I tried _____ into the marketing class, but I wasn't able to.

    a. to get   b. getting   c. to getting

12. Jen is afraid _____ the international marketing class because her brother said it was difficult.

    a. take   b. to take   c. taking

13. It's easy _____ which marketing strategies work the best.

    a. to see   b. to seeing   c. for see

14. Don has the ability _____ ads for social networking sites.

    a. to create   b. creating   c. creates

15. I had _____ a salesperson, but I didn't want to do it.

    a. a chance being   b. a chance to be   c. a chance I am

Art Credits

Illustration

Bill Dickson: 29, 103, 204; **Ortelius Design:** 152; **Rob Schuster:** 11, 127 *(top)*, 195, 196, 202, 210, 221; **Matt Stevens:** 14, 26, 28, 34, 127 *(bottom)*, 128; **Richard Williams:** 19, 20, 186

Photography

2 ©Photodisc/Thinkstock; 5 *(t)* ©iStockphoto/Thinkstock; *(b)* ©iStockphoto/Thinkstock; 12 Weegee(Arthur Fellig)/International Center of Photography / Getty Images; 21 Marc Romanelli/Getty Images; 37 ©Lisa F. Young/Alamy; 48 ©Jack Hollingsworth/Photodisc/Thinkstock; 52 ©Leila Cutler/Alamy; 59 ©iStockphoto/Thinkstock; 80 *(l)* ©Andrew Twort / Alamy; *(r)* Rob Melnychuk/Digital Vision/Getty Images; 82 ©Photos.com/Thinkstock; 85 ©PETER DASILVA/Redux; 86 Gilles Mingasson/Getty Images; 94 ©iStockphoto.com/Bariscan Celik; 100 ©iStockphoto.com/Michael Bodmann; 110 ©Mary Evans/Everett Collection; 132 Andersen Ross/Blend Images/Getty Images; 142 Leland Bobbe/Stone /Getty Images; 150 ©Hemera/Thinkstock; 168 ©MONPIX/Alamy; 170 Yuji Kotani/The Image Bank/Getty Images; 176 ©Pablo Paul/Alamy; 177 ©Hemera/Thinkstock; 180 ©Fox Searchlight/Everett Collection; 222 Jonas Ingerstedt/Johner Images/Getty Images; 228 ©New Line Productions/Zuma Press